Contents

Executive Summary   vii

Foreword   ix

Acknowledgments   xi

Introduction and Overview   1

Historical Origins of HBCUs   5

Desegregation   11
The Language of Higher Education Desegregation   12
Pre-*Brown* Cases   12
Brown I and II   13
Brown and HBCUs   14
Post-*Brown* HBCU Rebuttal   14
Sanders v. *Ellington*   15
Knight v. *Alabama*   17
Fordice Cases   18
Post-*Fordice* to the Present   22

Students   27
College Choice   28
Gender   31
African American Males   35
African American Females   37
Campus Environments   38
Graduation and Outcomes   39

Presidential Leadership   43

Faculty and Governance Issues   47
Faculty Diversity   47
Critique of Governance   49
General Overview of Faculty Issues   51

Fundraising   55
A History of Fundraising   56
Alumni Giving   57
Educating Alumni Early   58
Issues of Infrastructure   59
Endowment Size   59

Federal and State Policy   61
Legislation   61
State Policies Toward HBCUs   69

Curriculum   73
Professional Fields   76
Graduate Work   78
Black Medical Schools and Medical Education   79
Engineering at HBCUs   80
Accreditation   82

Conclusion and Thoughts About the Future   85

Appendix: Historically Black Colleges and Universities   89

References   93

Additional Readings   107

Name Index   121

Subject Index   126

About the Authors   133

Executive Summary

Born out of extreme racism and shepherded through the centuries by endur-
ing hope, the nation's historically black colleges and universities (HBCUs)
have educated countless African Americans. These institutions, which boast
great diversity, are treasures that illuminate the talent and potential of African
Americans. This book provides an overview of the salient issues facing HBCUs
as well as the many contributions that these historic institutions make to our
country as a whole. The book is organized into nine chapters, discussing a historical overview of HBCUs, examining their founding as well as the role of
African Americans, missionaries, and industrial philanthropists in their development. It also looks at how these institutions have changed over time.
It delves deeply into the controversial topic of desegregation, offering various
perspectives on the issue and showing how the courts have treated HBCUs in
the post-*Brown* era. It examines issues pertaining to students, the area about
which the most research has been completed, including college choice, retention, graduation rates, and issues of gender and student engagement. The fourth
chapter focuses on presidential leadership over time. Although this topic is
vitally important, it has not been adequately covered by scholars researching
HBCUs. The book also focuses on faculty, and considers governance issues,
including the limited research on the subject; it considers whether the unique
context of HBCUs makes a difference in the role of shared governance. The
book also highlights fundraising issues at HBCUs, giving attention to a vitally
important area that needs additional consideration from scholars. It explores
the history and current status of fundraising at HBCUs, alumni giving practices, and gaps in the literature. The book also looks at the role of federal and

state policy as it pertains to HBCUs, examining the impact of various legislation and practices. It continues by investigating issues pertaining to the curriculum, exploring changes in the foci of curricula and their impact on students, and it offers some concluding thoughts with future areas of exploration for researchers.

Foreword

President Obama has placed several remarkable challenges before the higher education community and the nation: to offer a college education to every qualified student, regardless of income, and to have the highest proportion of students graduating from college in the world by 2020. Meeting these challenges will require the commitment and resources of the nation's HBCUs to serve the increased pipeline of students needed to meet the president's goal.

We welcome this challenge, not because it won't be difficult—it will—but because we have a long history of successfully educating an academically diverse student body.

But to move forward, we need to know where we have been and where we stand at this critical crossroads in history—preparing academically and globally competitive students. In this concise yet comprehensive volume, Professor Marybeth Gasman and her coauthors provide those answers—from the history and evolution of HBCUs to the successes and struggles of the present day.

Unearthing Promise and Potential: Our Nation's Historically Black Colleges and Universities is an invaluable publication that belongs on the bookshelves of anyone working, teaching, or learning in higher education—or who simply wishes to become more knowledgeable about the great American story of the HBCU mission and experience.

The authors summarize the evolution of HBCUs, from their pre–Civil War and land-grant origins in the era of segregation to their contemporary efforts to provide educational opportunities for African Americans and other poor and minority students in a time of increasing diversity and financial pressures.

But they have done more by distilling the vast amount of research that has been conducted on HBCUs. Professor Gasman and her colleagues may not have read everything worth reading about HBCUs, but they have come close. The authors' citations, reference list, and suggestions for further research constitute a valuable resource that will give students and researchers alike opportunities for investigating the story of American education and the role that HBCUs play in it.

This book examines such milestones as the second Morrill Act of 1890, the debate between industrial training versus liberal arts education personified by Booker T. Washington and W.E.B. Du Bois, the struggles against segregation and racism, and the impact of *Brown* v. *Board of Education* in 1954 and the Higher Education Act of 1965.

It explores a panoply of contemporary issues facing HBCUs as well: recruitment, retention, and graduation rates; education in science and engineering, teaching, and medicine; gender and diversity; financial stability and government support; endowments and fundraising; and accreditation and governance. For the generalist and the scholar, *Unearthing Promise and Potential* is an invaluable resource in understanding where we stand as we seek to advance our educational goals for students of color throughout the United States.

In the words of President Obama, "Education is no longer just a pathway to opportunity and success, it is a prerequisite to success."

Acknowledgments

Writing a monograph always involves many individuals who provide support and encouragement throughout the process. First, I am grateful to Lisa Wolf-Wendel and Kelly Ward, the editors of the Association for the Study of Higher Education's monograph series. Lisa solicited this monograph, and although I was covered with writing projects when she asked, the topic was of such importance that I said "yes." I said yes for two specific reasons. First, having a short, succinct publication on historically black colleges and universities that can easily be used in classes or as a first point of reference is crucial to expanding the knowledge of those in the academy and beyond about these important institutions. I saw writing this monograph as an opportunity to work with some of my students and colleagues. I feel very strongly about giving young scholars and practitioners opportunities to conduct research and write, and this was a great occasion to do it. As such, I asked three people to coauthor this monograph. Valerie Lundy-Wagner, a Ph.D. candidate at the University of Pennsylvania, served as my research assistant for several years. We have written a number of quantitative articles related to HBCUs together—and it has certainly broadened my horizons. Valerie's well-honed research skills made for rich contributions to this book. I also asked Tafaya Ransom, a Hampton University graduate and a brand-new Ph.D. student at the University of Pennsylvania. Tafaya currently serves as my research assistant, and I have the privilege of being her advisor. She is interested in curriculum issues and engineering education at HBCUs. Of note, Tafaya contributed her parts to the monograph before she was officially a Penn student, demonstrating her dedication and enthusiasm for the project. Last, I asked Nelson Bowman III, a Morehouse College graduate and director of development at Prairie View A&M University. I met Nelson a few years ago at a fundraising conference and was immediately impressed with his thirst for knowledge and curiosity. I asked him to participate in this project because of his experience working at an HBCU and his understanding of fundraising in the HBCU context. Moreover, I thought that Nelson could help us maintain "realness" in the monograph, which would make it accessible to both researchers and practitioners. Because of these three individuals, this project has been a joy! I look forward to working more with each of the coauthors in the future and thank them for their dedication, sense of humor, and professionalism throughout the duration of this project.

I would personally like to thank Edward M. Epstein and sweet Chloe S. Epstein for their support of me during the writing of this mongraph and always. Chloe, in particular, reminds me each day why life is so very worth living.

Marybeth Gasman

I would like to graciously thank my entire extended family, especially my mother, Pamela Stewart Wagner, who has provided me with inspiration every day of my life and always exemplifies the meaning of strength and perseverance. I am also forever indebted to Kahlil Gibran Fitzgerald, for helping me realize ten years ago that faith in oneself is rarely found in a book, but in people. Finally, I would like to acknowledge the many people who support me, including Marybeth Gasman, Laura Perna, Christopher L. Tudico, H. Isabella Lanza, and my longtime ABC family.

Valerie Lundy-Wagner

I am extremely grateful to my family for their unwavering support and constant inspiration, particularly my mother, sister, and brother—Rhonda Grier, Shanee Franks, and Paul Ransom. I would also like to thank Sharon and Clarence Grier, who have by their example and guidance, helped me in countless ways. Finally, I am grateful to Marybeth Gasman for including me on this project as well as my colleagues and mentors at the University of Pennsylvania, the University of Michigan, and Hampton University.

Tafaya Ransom

When I accepted the invitation to coauthor this monograph, I knew I would be pushed far beyond the boundaries of my comfort zone. Now that the project is complete, I am glad I faced my fear and did it. I would like to thank my parents, especially my mom, who is no longer of this earth but I know watches me from above. I also want to thank my loving wife, Michelle, who has stood by me through thick and thin and always tells me what a wonderful man I am. My son Kyle, who when told of this project said, "Oh so you're an author now?" also deserves thanks. Last but not least, I want to thank my friend and mentor Marybeth Gasman, who saw my potential and brought it to the surface just as she has done with countless others. Thank you so much for the opportunity.

Nelson Bowman III

Published online in Wiley InterScience
(www.interscience.wiley.com) • DOI: 10.1002/aehe.3505

Introduction and Overview

THE YEAR 2008 MARKED A HISTORIC ACHIEVEMENT in the events of the United States: we the people elected an African American man to the presidency of our nation. Even though President Barack Obama did not attend a historically black college or university (HBCU), these institutions and their graduates have had a great impact on this man and his life. Black colleges have played a significant role in building the African American middle class in the United States, educating individuals who are the nation's politicians, doctors, teachers, judges, scientists, professors, and business leaders. These individuals have worked tirelessly to change the racial climate in the United States in a way that has made it possible for Barack Obama to succeed.

According to Joy Williamson in *Radicalizing the Ebony Tower* (2008), black colleges served as movement centers for the black freedom struggle, educating students who risked their lives in support of equality for all Americans. Without the efforts of these students and the faculty and administrators at black colleges who supported them, Barack Obama would have been hard pressed to secure the Democratic nomination. Black colleges also have a legacy of encouraging civic engagement and community organizing—a legacy upon which President Obama capitalized. He used community organizing—a tradition that has been nurtured by black colleges and the black church—to create a movement for change in the United States.

The election of the first African American president leads one to wonder about the future of HBCUs. For those watching and listening to President Obama, it is apparent that, although he acknowledges societal and systemic racism, he also promotes individual responsibility—hewing a middle path between the perspectives of left and right. When Obama's ideas are applied to the context of HBCUs, one gets a pragmatic, success-oriented approach to education. He is not interested in hearing about the reasons HBCUs cannot succeed but the ways they can thrive. President Obama is not a product of the civil rights movement in a traditional sense and as such is not as focused on supporting and sustaining institutions such as HBCUs merely because it is the right or moral thing to do. It is our belief that our president is wholeheartedly committed to social justice, but we also know that he is a pragmatist who consistently puts policy and action above politics. If one listens closely, it seems that President Obama believes the only way for HBCUs to thrive and excel in the current economic and social environment is to focus on increasing degree attainment and other student outcomes. HBCUs need to show, in measurable ways, that they are adding considerable value to the lives and livelihood of their students.

The nation's HBCUs are diverse. Although we discuss them as a category based on their historical racial makeup, these institutions are in fact quite different from one another. According to the government's definition, HBCUs are bound together by the fact that they were established before 1964 (the year of the Civil Rights Act) with the express purpose of educating African Americans. These institutions, of which there are 105, are public, private, large, small, religious, nonsectarian, selective, and open. They educate just over three hundred thousand students. Some HBCUs are thriving, others are barely making ends meet, and most fall in between. Regardless, most HBCUs provide a much needed education to African American students (and many others).

HBCUs were created during the decades after the Civil War to educate the newly freed black population (three exceptions being Cheyney University of Pennsylvania, Lincoln University, and Wilberforce University, which were all created before 1861). The majority of private HBCUs were established by both black and white missionary organizations aiming to Christianize the former slaves. On the other hand, the bulk of the nation's public HBCUs were the result of the second Morrill Act of 1890. Southern state governments were not willing to integrate their historically white institutions (HWIs) but still wanted federal funding for higher education; as such, they established a separate group of black institutions. Through the 1970s, these institutions, both public and private, were responsible for graduating the lion's share of African Americans in the United States. Currently, HBCUs enroll 16 percent and graduate approximately 20 percent of all African Americans who attend college. Although their enrollments have steadied in recent years, HBCUs continue to compete with better resourced historically white institutions for students. The main draw to HBCUs for African American students is the empowering, family-like environment that boasts small classes, close faculty-student relationships, and life with fewer racial microaggressions.

Throughout these introductory comments, we allude to many important issues, noting how these issues are manifest in the HBCU environment. With this book we hope to provide a broad overview of HBCUs, surveying the state of research and also providing our perspective on the state of practice in these institutions. We should note that our aim is not to delve deeply into subject areas or to provide new research; instead, we bring together a large body of research, critiquing and organizing it, and pointing to the holes in the research. We hope this book will entice readers to consider reading more and possibly pursuing much needed research on the various facets of HBCUs.

The book is organized into nine chapters. First we provide a historical overview of HBCUs, examining their founding as well as the role of African Americans, missionaries, and industrial philanthropists in their development. We also look at how these institutions have changed over time, given the many developments in the United States over the course of their existence. The second chapter delves deeply into the controversial topic of desegregation, offering various perspectives on the issue and showing how the courts have treated HBCUs in the post-*Brown* era. The third chapter examines issues pertaining to students, the area about which the most research has been completed. We explore college choice, retention, and graduation rates as well as issues of gender and student engagement. The fourth chapter focuses on presidential leadership over time. Although this topic is vitally important, it has not been adequately covered by scholars researching HBCUs. In many ways connected to the subject of presidential leadership, the fifth chapter focuses on faculty and governance issues. It looks at the limited research on the subject and also considers whether the specific context of HBCUs makes a difference in the role of shared governance. The sixth chapter highlights fundraising issues at

HBCUs, giving attention to a vitally important area that needs additional consideration from scholars. It explores the history and current status of fundraising at HBCUs, alumni giving practices, and gaps in the literature. The next chapter looks at the role of federal and state policy as it pertains to HBCUs, examining the impact of various legislation and practices. The eighth chapter investigates issues pertaining to the curriculum, exploring changes in the foci of curriculum and their impact on students. And the final chapter offers some concluding thoughts as well as future areas of exploration for researchers. An appendix lists HBCUs in the United States today.

Historical Origins of HBCUs

$\mathbf{F}$ROM THEIR ARRIVAL ON THE SHORES of the United States, black people have thirsted for knowledge and viewed education as the key to their freedom. These enslaved people pursued various forms of education despite laws, in all southern states, barring them from learning to read and write. In the North, free blacks pursued education at three colleges for African Americans: Lincoln and Cheyney Universities in Pennsylvania and Wilberforce University in Ohio. With the end of the Civil War, the enormous task of educating more than four million African Americans was shouldered by the federal government, through the Freedman's Bureau, and many northern church missionaries. As early as 1865, the Freedmen's Bureau began establishing HBCUs, resulting in mainly male staff and teachers with military backgrounds. During the post–Civil War period, most HBCUs were so in name only; these institutions generally provided primary and secondary education during the first decades of their existence.

As noted, religious missionary organizations—some affiliated with northern white denominations such as the Baptists and Congregationalists and some with black churches such as the African Methodist Episcopalians—actively worked with the Freedmen's Bureau. One of the most prominent white organizations was the American Missionary Association, but there were many others as well. White northern missionary societies founded HBCUs such as Dillard University in New Orleans and Morehouse College in Atlanta. The benevolence of these missionaries was tinged with self-interest and often racism. The missionaries' goals in establishing these colleges were to Christianize the freedmen (that is, convert formerly enslaved people to·their brand of Christianity) and to rid the country of the "menace" of uneducated African Americans (Anderson, 1988). Among the colleges founded by black denominations were Morris Brown College in Atlanta, Paul Quinn College in Dallas, and Allen University in Columbia, South Carolina. Distinctive among American colleges, these institutions were founded *by* African Americans *for* African Americans (Anderson, 1988). Because these institutions relied on less support from whites and more support from black churches, they were able to design their own curricula; however, they also were more vulnerable to economic instability and continue to be currently.

With the passage of the second Morrill Act in 1890, the federal government again took an interest in black education, establishing public black colleges. This act stipulated that those states practicing segregation in their public colleges and universities would forfeit federal funding unless they established agricultural and mechanical institutions for the black population (Gasman, 2007a; Thompson, 1973). Despite the wording of the Morrill Act, which called for the equitable division of federal funds, these newly founded institutions received considerably less funding than their white counterparts and thus had inferior facilities and more limited course offerings. Among the seventeen new "land-grant" colleges were Prairie View A&M and North Carolina A&T Universities.

By the close of the nineteenth century, private black colleges had used up the limited funding from missionary philanthropists. At roughly the same time, a new kind of philanthropic support materialized—white northern industrial philanthropy. Among the businessmen who provided this philanthropic support were Andrew Carnegie, James Baldwin, John D. Rockefeller, Julius Rosenwald, and John Foster Peabody. These industry leaders, motivated by a desire to control the various forms of industry, possessed a hint of Christian benevolence (Anderson, 1988; Watkins, 2001). The organization making the most significant contribution to African American higher education was the General Education Board, a collection of white philanthropists created by John D. Rockefeller, Sr., but led by John D. Rockefeller, Jr. Over the first half of the twentieth century, the board gave roughly $63 million to black higher education, a remarkable figure but only a fraction of what it provided to white colleges and universities (Anderson, 1988). Despite their personal agendas, the funding structure that these industrial giants created was designed in part to control black education in ways that would benefit the industrial philanthropists by producing graduates skilled in the trades that served the industrialists' enterprises (Anderson, 1988; Watkins, 2001). In particular, the colleges and universities they supported were exceptionally vigilant not to disturb the segregationists' system of racism that ruled the South by the 1890s. Black institutions such as Hampton and Tuskegee were hallmarks of industrial education. It was at these types of institutions that young African Americans were taught how to shoe horses, sew, cook, and clean under the tutelage of men such as Samuel Chapman Armstrong at Hampton and his protégé Booker T. Washington at Tuskegee.

Of note, many African American intellectuals opposed the philanthropists' support of industrial education, favoring instead a liberal arts curriculum. Institutions such as Fisk, Dillard, Howard, Spelman, and Morehouse, for example, were more representative of the liberal arts curriculum advocated by W.E.B. Du Bois than of Booker T. Washington's philosophy of advancement through labor and self-sufficiency. Despite the philosophical differences between Washington and Du Bois, the two men both had a goal of educating blacks and uplifting African Americans as a whole. Basically, Washington favored educating blacks in the industrial arts so they might become economically self-sufficient, whereas Du Bois wanted to create a black intellectual elite or "talented tenth" to lead the race toward overall autonomy (Gasman, Baez, and Turner, 2008).

In 1915, the attitudes of the northern philanthropists changed; they began to shift their attention and funding toward those black institutions that focused on the liberal arts. Realizing that industrial education could exist alongside a liberal arts curriculum, the philanthropists chose to lend their support more broadly to black higher education institutions (Anderson, 1988). The omnipresent power of industrial philanthropy in the early twentieth century led to conservative campuses at black colleges—campuses that would often tolerate only those presidents and leaders (for the most part white men) who supported or accommodated segregation. Of note, attention from the philanthropists was not especially welcomed by universities such as Fisk, where rebellions broke out against tyrannical leaders whom students labeled puppets of the white philanthropists (Anderson, 1988; Gasman, Baez, and Turner, 2008). Despite these conflicts, industrial philanthropists provided major support for private black colleges until the late 1930s.

By this time, the white philanthropists had begun to focus their attention elsewhere, providing only scant funding to HBCUs (Gasman, 2008a). In response, Frederick D. Patterson, who at the time was president of the Tuskegee Institute, recommended that the country's private black colleges join forces in their fundraising labors. As a result, in 1944, the leaders of 29 black colleges and universities came together to create the United Negro College Fund. The fund began solely as a fundraising organization, but over time it took on advocacy and educational roles as well (Gasman, 2004, 2008a; Gasman, Baez, and Turner, 2008).

Both public and private black colleges in the South remained segregated by law and were the only educational option for African Americans until *Brown* v. *Board of Education* in 1954. Although most institutions of higher education did not experience the same violent fallout from the *Brown* decision as southern public schools, they were greatly influenced by the decision. The Supreme Court's ruling meant that HBCUs would be placed in competition with white institutions when recruiting African American students. With the end of legal segregation in *Brown,* many white liberals and some blacks began to question the future of HBCUs and refer to them as vestiges of segregation (Gasman, 2008a). Desegregation proceeded slowly, however, with many public HBCUs and historically white institutions maintaining their racial concentrations even today.

After the *Brown* decision, private HBCUs, which have always been willing to accept students from all backgrounds if the law would allow, struggled to defend issues of quality in an atmosphere that labeled anything all-black inferior (Gasman, 2008a). Many black colleges also suffered from "brain drain" as predominately white institutions in the North and some in the South made efforts to attract high-achieving black students once racial diversity became valued in higher education (Gasman, 2008a).

The black college of the 1960s was a much different place from that of the 1920s. The leadership switched from white to black, and because blacks had more control over funding, dissent and black self-determination among the student population were better tolerated (Gasman, 2008a; Williamson, 2008). On many public and private black college campuses throughout the South, students staged sit-ins and protested against segregation and its manifestations throughout the region (Williamson, 2008). Most prominent perhaps were the four students from North Carolina A&T who refused to leave a segregated Woolworth lunch counter in 1960. As Williamson (2008) argues, these student activist were valiant in their fight for civil rights.

During the 1960s the federal government took a greater interest in black colleges. In an attempt to provide clarity, the Higher Education Act of 1965 defined a black college as "any . . . college or university that was established prior to 1964, whose principal mission was, and is, the education of black Americans." The recognition of the uniqueness of black colleges implied in this definition has led to increased federal funding for these institutions.

Another federal intervention on behalf of black colleges took place in 1980, when President Jimmy Carter signed Executive Order 12232 establishing a national program to alleviate the effects of discriminatory treatment and to strengthen and expand black colleges to provide quality education. Since then, every U.S. president has renewed the commitment to black colleges set forth by Carter through this program.

The history of HBCUs continues to shape these institutions in meaningful and positive ways; however, this history also confines HBCUs from time to time. Often when outsiders are familiar only with the history of HBCUs, they fail to see what is currently happening, including these institutions' service to diverse constituencies, their enormous track record in the sciences, and their continuing and crucial role in educating those African Americans who eventually occupy the black middle class. The subsequent chapters discuss the changing role of HBCUs, their strengths and weaknesses, and areas that need attention from researchers and practitioners alike.

Desegregation

B EFORE 1954, policies that upheld and enforced segregation in education and other arenas were legally mandated (*de jure*) in the United States.
(*De jure* segregation refers to segregation designated by law, whereas *de facto*
segregation refers to segregation that happens in practice.) In the case of black
American higher education, segregation policies stem largely from the Hatch
Act of 1877 and the second Morrill Act of 1890 (Brady, Eatman, and Parker,
2000). Though these pieces of legislation included provisions to develop and
fund HBCUs typically in specific academic fields (such as agriculture, mechanical arts, and English), these policies omitted the notion of equality in educational opportunity. States were given the choice either to show that race was
not an admissions criterion in schools or to designate a separate land-grant
institution for black students. Of the nineteen southern and border states, all
opted to establish separate systems of higher education between 1890 and
1899, resulting in at least one public HBCU planned or chartered each year
during that period (M. C. Brown, 2001).

In the fifty years since *Brown,* various judicial acts have served to bolster,
defeat, and confuse the role of HBCUs in American higher education. A few
important cases are briefly reviewed here to provide a glimpse of the shifts in
how HBCUs have been addressed. An important consideration in the cases
noted here, as well as those unmentioned, pertains to the rulings on elementary and secondary schools and how they ought to be applied in the postsecondary arena, namely school choice and equal educational opportunity
(Ware, 1994).

The Language of Higher Education Desegregation

The language of higher education desegregation is often confused, misused, or misrepresented, especially when used to describe HBCUs (M. C. Brown, 2001; Williamson, 2004a; Richardson and Harris, 2004). In fact, terms like *segregation, integration, separation, color blindness, racial neutrality,* and *race consciousness* have largely remained undefined in public, political, and legal arenas. This ambiguity has played an important role in the evolution of higher education desegregation, as these terms coincide at least loosely with paradigm shifts.

For the purpose of this chapter, these terms are associated with desegregation:

Desegregation—Provisions articulated in law or practice that eliminate the isolation of members of a particular group into separate functional units (Richardson and Harris, 2004, p. 366)

Segregation—Provisions to compel the separation of individuals and groups

Integration—Provisions to compel the incorporation of individuals and groups as equals in society

Race neutral—Provisions that afford neither majority nor minority groups an advantage (also known as color blind)

Race conscious—Provisions that acknowledge differences in minority and majority groups to inform policymaking

Pre-*Brown* Cases

Before the *Brown* cases, the focus of desegregation in higher education addressed access to graduate and professional schools (see *Missouri ex rel. Gaines* v. *Canada* [305 U.S. 337 (1938)], *Sipuel* v. *Board of Regents of Univ. of Okla.* [332 U.S. 631 (1948)], and *Sweatt* v. *Painter* [339 U.S. 629 (1950)], for example). In general, most states had appropriated funding and facilities—however inferior—toward the development of undergraduate education only (Ware, 1994). With leadership from the NAACP and relative judicial success, these cases marked the first Supreme Court–ordered admission of an African

American student into a postsecondary institution and laid a foundation from which to engage in *Brown* (Ware, 1994).

Brown I and II

Although African Americans are on record as challenging racial segregation (and thereby calling for racial integration) in schools as early as 1894 (see *Roberts v. Boston* [59 Mass. (5 Cush.) 198 (1850]), the *Brown v. Board of Education of Topeka* [347 U.S. 483 (1954)] ruling is generally considered the catalyst for ending the "separate but equal" status quo. Comprising court cases from Delaware, Kansas, South Carolina, Virginia, and Washington, D.C., in effect, this first ruling declared that racial segregation in public spheres was unconstitutional. This unanimous Supreme Court decision declared that separate educational facilities were inherently unequal and violated the Fourteenth Amendment of the U.S. Constitution, specifically the Equal Protection Clause.

The May 17, 1954, ruling, however, was met with a considerable backlash of apathy toward racial integration at HWIs and individual and institutional defiance. Approximately one year later, in response to the de facto segregation, schools in jurisdictions covered in *Brown I* were brought to the Supreme Court again in what is often referred to as *Brown II*. In this second ruling, the Court delegated the task of (white) school desegregation and called for "deliberate speed." Still, the calls for expediency were met with antipathy, as the school systems that had been running racially separate school systems were curiously expected to correct their own previously unequal conditions (F. V. Baxter, 1982). It was not until 1962 that the first African American student was admitted to the University of Mississippi by the court decree (M. C. Brown, 2001; Ware, 1994). Despite these changes in policy, however, many institutions at all levels remained racially isolated as a result of other societal remnants of de jure segregation such as racially derived housing patterns (Ware, 1994). In 1958, the ensuing desegregation efforts had not had a significant impact on HBCUs (Jenkins, 1958).

The *Brown* rulings represented two legal theoretical principles: educational opportunity based on race was inherently unequal, and unequal opportunity was pervasive in American educational institutions. With respect to the first principle, the Court ruled that the maintenance of race-based exclusion was illegal, paving the way for black integration of HWIs. Second, the Court acknowledged that African Americans were entitled to equal educational opportunity commensurate with their white peers, which meant that equality in funding, infrastructure, and quality of education, for example, was necessary. At the time, the *Brown* ruling was viewed as the Court's support for the maintenance of HBCUs, as it provided African Americans access to postsecondary education (Ware, 1994). Further, because HBCUs supported African American educational opportunity, the responsibility fell to the states to distribute resources equitably. Although neither mandated nor explicitly stated, white integration of HBCUs was also implicit in the rulings.

Brown and HBCUs

Because the *Brown* rulings addressed African Americans' entrée into white educational arenas, the mandate to desegregate higher education fell largely on HWIs. Shortly after the *Brown* rulings, however, the United Negro College Fund and other HBCU advocates prepared for and announced strategic use of HBCUs in the HWI-focused desegregation process (Gasman, 2008a). Not considering HBCUs as segregating institutions and recognizing that social backlash was imminent in terms of black integration at HWIs, HBCUs were offered as the natural mechanism for transition (Jenkins, 1958; Gasman, 2008a). In effect, this maneuvering implied that HBCUs would play a long-term but necessary role in the desegregation of American higher education.

Not surprisingly, problems with consensus in terms of policy development, evaluation, and modification at HWIs contribute to what early twenty-first-century scholars contend is the continued segregation of American higher education (Baxter, 1982; Harley, 2001; Williamson, 2008). Although *Brown* represented a conceptual triumph for African American educational opportunity, subsequent judicial rulings have detracted policymaking away from the promotion of equal educational opportunity.

Post-*Brown* HBCU Rebuttal

Although advocates saw the post-*Brown* era as a unique place for HBCUs in the social, educational, and judicial arenas, challengers were able to champion their own wins using both language and shifts in legal argumentation. In fact, HBCU antagonists were able to use various power structures (state and local government, higher education boards, and the judiciary, for example) to expose the Supreme Court's lack of will to actively participate in explicitly race-related education and public policymaking (Baxter, 1982). Interestingly, these were the same power structures that until 1954 had attempted to thwart equal educational opportunity for African Americans and other marginalized groups, and this precarious fact has not gone unnoticed by critics of the Supreme Court's post-*Brown* treatment of HBCUs (Brady, Eatman, and Parker, 2000; Ware, 1994).

Sanders v. Ellington

Sanders v. *Ellington* [288 F. Supp. 937 (1968)] was filed by then law student and part-time faculty member at the University of Tennessee, Rita Sanders, against the state and federal governments. Sanders (now Sanders Geier) argued that the late 1960s expansion of the predominately white, part-time, two-year night school programs at the University of Tennessee–Nashville (UT–Nashville) to four-year programs encroached on the ability of the four-year historically black Tennessee Agricultural and Industrial State University (TAISU, now known as Tennessee State University or TSU) to desegregate. That is, the expansion of UT–Nashville was anticipated to undermine TAISU's efforts three miles away to attract more white (and nonblack) students and faculty. With the support of the U.S. Department of Justice, Sanders Geier was successful in blocking the expansion of UT–Nashville, and the court ordered a desegregation plan for Tennessee's public system of higher education.

Although the state provided encouraging updates on the enrollment and employment at its public institutions by race, a desegregation plan was never developed. As a result, in 1972 a judge ordered TSU to increase white enrollment, making no mention of the state's predominately white institutions and their role in desegregation. Under the philosophy of separate and unequal, the court ruled that without an increase in white enrollment and employment, TAISU would remain inferior (Baxter, 1982). This one-sided approach to integration, both philosophically and legally, was met with a suit by predominately black TSU students and staff (with assistance from the NAACP Legal Defense and Education Fund), who argued that too much emphasis was placed on ridding TSU of its historical albeit racial history and too little on Tennessee's historically white institutions. The earlier rulings represented a departure from identifying societal discrimination to state-support and implementation of de jure segregation.

Eleven years after the initial case, a merger of TSU and UT–Nashville was proposed, a suggestion that eventually came to fruition. Unlike prior mergers of predominately white and historically black institutions, it was the first time a majority campus was dissolved into a historically black institution. The resulting institution, Tennessee State University, faced many challenges initially, including UT–Nashville students' refusal to enroll in TSU and fights over academic department control from faculty at both institutions. For years this merger languished, until 1983, when a group of predominately white faculty at TSU (originally from UT–Nashville) sought to ensure that the institution's policies and practices were conducive to the continued desegregation of TSU. It resulted in a plan in which academic programs and facilities at TSU would be improved, which also mentioned the need for a statewide plan for integration of state institutions of higher education.

Although the plan was established, the state did little to assure its implementation, and in 1990 TSU students engaged in a hunger strike to protest dormitory conditions. The media attention led to then-Governor McWherter's visit to the campus and eventual appropriation of $127 million to renovate and construct new buildings at TSU. Unfortunately, this effort was met with little enthusiasm. During this time, the *Fordice* case helped Sanders Grier's in that it upheld the maintenance of publicly supported HBCUs in the early 1990s; however, TSU supporters were not satisfied with this philosophical win. Eventually, all parties signed a consent decree in January 2001, (1) eliminating the use of numerical quotas in enrollment and employment at public institutions, (2) enhancing academic program offerings in the Nashville campus (now named the Avon Williams Campus), (3) providing $23 million for renovations and developing scholarships for TSU, and (4) establishing policies for improving cross-racial enrollment and employment. In the five years after the decree, approximately $77 million was spent on improvements to

TSU. The only academic program loss of the decree was the purchase of Nashville School of Law; however, the $10 million allocated to that program was redirected. The original and subsequent suits were all dropped in 2006 when the state of Tennessee was determined to have completed its obligations to integrate the public system of higher education. Although the merger and allocation of funds to TSU was positive, some argue that the lack of court supervision in maintaining desegregated higher education proves challenging.

Knight v. Alabama

The *Knight* cases represented a major blow to HBCUs in the higher education desegregation movement, with the court's turning its attention away from simply equal educational opportunity (Brooks, 2004). In what eventually was a set of cases, John F. Knight and other alumni of historically black Alabama State University alleged that duplicative programs and services of two nearby state-supported HWI branch campuses (Auburn and Troy State Universities) inhibited the white desegregation of their HBCU alma mater (Brooks, 2004; Ware, 1994). The suit identified three issues considered to maintain remnants of de jure segregation: unequal resource allocation, noncompliance in the creation of HBCUs as flagship institutions, and denial of federal funds (Brooks, 2004). Although *Knight* v. *Alabama* is still being litigated in the federal district court, it has had an impact on HBCUs.

Nearly ten years after first filing suit, Alabama was charged with maintaining *de facto* segregation in its higher education system. Although this charge validated the plaintiffs' position, the ruling also mandated that the state seek "to eliminate all vestiges of segregation" (Brooks, 2004, p. 352), which applied to Alabama's HWIs and HBCUs alike. The explicit attack on HBCUs is well noted in the court's pronouncement that HBCUs have failed to attract white students and to appoint and retain white faculty. Whereas in *Brown* HBCUs were not mandated to act, this ruling clearly required action.

In addition, the ruling ordered an improvement in the quality of HBCUs by requiring Alabama's HBCUs to increase their endowments, establish new academic programs, provide white and other nonblack students with scholarship opportunities, participate in program consolidation with HWIs, and identify and implement recruitment strategies for whites (Brooks, 2004). Although the *Knight* ruling also required the state of Alabama to act, the decision departed explicitly from the understanding that HBCUs were established in reaction to *de jure* segregation to the notion that HBCUs were colluders in state-sanctioned de facto segregation. By comparing the two institutional types, the court suggested that HBCUs eliminate their black character (through enrollment and employment) to remedy *de jure* segregation and treat HBCUs and HWIs similarly.

In the end, the *Knight* case exemplifies a major departure from *Brown* in its focus on HBCUs as racially identifiable in an exclusionary sense rather than from a historical perspective of inclusion and equal educational opportunity (Brooks, 2004; Ware, 1994). This new paradigm set a standard in which HBCUs were more explicitly addressed and susceptible to attack through judicial and legislative arenas.

Fordice Cases

In 1992, the U.S. Supreme Court handed down a decision in the long-litigated case *United States* v. *Fordice* [112 S. Ct. 2727], first filed in 1975 by African American James Ayers on behalf of his son, a student at Jackson State University in Mississippi. Its ruling required states to eliminate policies that perpetuated segregation among their public colleges. As part of that decision, the Court returned the case to the federal district court (whose earlier decision, declaring that Mississippi had fulfilled its obligations of desegregation, was overturned by the Supreme Court) to determine specific remedies for the ongoing inequities in that state.

In 1995, the federal district court issued a ruling intended to remove overt racial classifications from the state's eight public universities. Steps to be taken included standardizing the admissions requirements across all eight schools (previously, the five historically white institutions had stricter standards than the three historically black universities) and enacting policies to ensure a certain minimum racial diversity at each university. The plaintiffs and the U.S. Department of Justice appealed this ruling to the U.S. Court of Appeals for the Fifth Circuit. In 1997, the Fifth Circuit ordered the federal court judge to reconsider parts of this 1995 ruling but upheld the new admissions standards. This decision was then appealed to the U.S. Supreme Court, which in 1998 refused without comment to hear the case. In 2001, after months of negotiations, all parties agreed to a $503 million settlement. The federal court approved the settlement in 2002. Later that year, some of the plaintiffs appealed the settlement in federal court, arguing that it did not go far enough to remedy the effects of segregation. When this appeal was denied, the plaintiffs appealed to the Fifth Circuit, which in late January 2004 issued its rejection of all counts of the appeal. In May 2004, the case was appealed to the U.S. Supreme Court, which in October refused, without comment, to hear the case, thus ending the thirty-year legal battle and rendering the 2002 settlement legally binding.

The $503 million settlement is to be distributed over seventeen years and is earmarked for Mississippi's three public historically black institutions: Alcorn State, Jackson State, and Mississippi Valley State. The largest amount is to be used to enhance programs and facilities at those universities. A smaller portion will provide funds to allow a greater number of financially strapped students to enroll in summer and remedial programs. Just under one-fifth of the total settlement is to be used by the three universities in efforts to recruit nonblack students. The court set a goal for each of them to achieve a nonblack enrollment of at least 10 percent, a requirement they must meet for three consecutive years before gaining direct control of the funds earmarked for recruiting nonblack students. The terms of this agreement apply to only the three historically black universities in Mississippi, as the five historically white universities have surpassed the minimum of 10 percent for nonwhite enrollment.

The plaintiffs who appealed the settlement argue that it focuses unfairly on black institutions, forcing them to integrate when they have more urgent financial needs. They also argue that the settlement, while seemingly generous, in reality provides little money to correct decades-long injustices. They further object that the standardized admissions practices involved effectively bar thousands of black students from enrolling in college. The plaintiffs wanted the mission and programs of the black universities to be significantly expanded as part of the settlement, but the federal court refused to consider that issue as central to the settlement. The Fifth Circuit rejected every aspect of the plaintiffs' appeal, noting that "this litigation concerns eliminating the effects of prior legal segregation, not mandating equality among Mississippi's publicly funded educational institutions" (Weerts and Conrad, 2002, p. 36).

Reaction to the final settlement was mixed. Leaders of Alcorn State, Jackson State, and Mississippi Valley State all expressed eagerness to have the case closed and to move forward with planned improvements to their campuses with the money earmarked for that purpose in the settlements. Politicians, state leaders, and members of Mississippi's state board of education also expressed their satisfaction with the results of the case. Others, however, including the attorney and plaintiffs who carried the appeal to the Supreme Court as well as professors and other leaders in Mississippi education, have expressed dismay over the outcome. They note the irony of the federal government's prohibiting admissions based on quantifiable "affirmative action" (designed to increase black participation at historically white schools) yet requiring public black universities to spend public money to recruit a preset number of nonblack students. They also object to the terms of the settlement that put the onus of integration on the three black universities, noting that the historically white schools' achievement of greater racial diversity is primarily because of their long histories of relative wealth and prestige. Furthermore, it is arguable whether the current level of desegregation at these traditionally white schools arises mainly from their own efforts or from those of students who insisted on their right to attend; the black colleges have certainly not tried to prevent nonblack students from attending their schools. Those who object to the final ruling in the case also point to the large population of black students in the state not served by any of the eight public universities, arguing that the three historically black colleges are uniquely situated to serve this population but that the current admissions standards prevent it. Overall, these plaintiffs—and supporters outside the state who have commented on the issue—believe that the settlement is a mere bandage over a deep wound and that the development of high-quality institutions to serve black students is further out of reach now than before the case was settled.

What implication does *Fordice* have for HBCUs and higher education over-all? The decades-long court case could result in additional resources given to black colleges to improve facilities if states continue to follow the spirit of the Court's decision. Critics contend, however, that this type of remedy for histor-ical discrimination by the state could, in fact, "slide back to the 'separate but equal' arrangement as defined by *Plessy* over a century ago" (Weerts and Con-rad, 2002, p. 37). Still, according to *Fordice* experts Weerts and Conrad (2002), "most observers concede that enhancement of the HBCUs is essential to level the playing field and to encourage students of all races to attend historically black institutions" (p. 37). Other outcomes of the *Fordice* decision might include increases in black college faculty salaries (making them comparable with those of their peers at predominantly white institutions) and the addition of new high quality master's and doctoral programs. Unfortunately, some state legislatures have suggested closure or the merging of black colleges with nearby predominantly white institutions (an action taken by the government in South Africa, a country that also had historically black institutions). According to Weerts and Conrad (2002), "most members of the black community continue to call this option an inappropriate remedy, pointing out the irony of closing the very institutions that sustained blacks during segregation as a way to com-bat the vestiges of segregation. Even after years of legal struggle, the question remains, will education for African Americans be improved?" (p. 38).

With regard to inequities in higher education, especially those addressed by *Fordice*, new research geared toward policymakers points to the continued inequality felt by African American students in the South. Of particular inter-est is a study that examined the status of equity for blacks in enrollment and bachelor's degree attainment at public institutions of higher education in the South (Perna and others, 2006). Perna and her colleagues found that despite some progress, public colleges and universities in the South remain greatly unequal for African Americans, with race being the strongest determinant of access and opportunity in higher education. The researchers also found that public four-year black colleges are the only sector of higher education in the South that consistently achieves equity in enrollment and degree completion across the nineteen southern and border states, whereas the greatest inequal-ity occurs at public flagship institutions.

Post-*Fordice* to the Present

Although *Fordice* has important direct implications for HBCUs—the rulings both supported and undermined their preservation—the case also helped to usher in an era that has been marked by anti–affirmative action sentiment in general. In fact, the focus on preserving African American equal educational opportunity has shifted toward protecting white students' educational opportunity and the continued neglect of other racial and ethnic groups. According to Adams (1986), support for affirmative action and the maintenance of public HBCUs was apparent in the initial aftermath of *Brown*: "the *Brown* Court did not indicate that single-race schools [that] do not discriminate in their admissions policies could never be legal" (p. 490). Rather, the focus of the *Brown* Court was to end a separate but equal education because of residual stigmatization of minority students.

Accordingly, Adams (1986) reminds HBCU proponents (and opponents) that such institutions could be considered remedial set-asides, which are only permissible under the Equal Protection Clause of the Fourteenth Amendment as a remedy for past discrimination. This option is permissible, however, only when consideration of reverse-racism against white students is taken and administrative, judicial, or legislative evidence of past or present constitutional or statutory violation under the Equal Protection Clause is provided. The idea to position some public HBCUs as remedial set-aside programs is clever and arguably necessary for their continued existence. Indeed, the use of affirmative action and associated rulings to bolster support for HBCUs may seem contradictory in light of the more recent rulings, yet the absence of such maneuvering would likely result in the virtual elimination of all public HBCUs (Adams, 1986).

In fact, the dissolution or elimination of many public HBCUs has been used as a remedy to integrate HWIs (Ware, 1994) and comply with Title VI of the Civil Rights Act of 1964. Consider, for example, if the state of Mississippi closed one public HBCU (Mississippi Valley State University) and merged another (Alcorn State University) with an HWI (Delta State University) as a compliance measure with respect to *Fordice*. This action would leave only one HBCU in Mississippi, Jackson State University. Although these actions may not seem catastrophic at face value, demographics and postsecondary educational opportunity, or lack thereof, suggest that African Americans in that state still suffer from de facto segregation.

Along these lines, consider that African Americans constitute more than one-third of the population in Mississippi, more than double that of the national average (U.S. Census Bureau, 2008). According to *Measuring Up* (2008), Mississippi is among the poorest-performing states in terms of high school completion, which affects the extremely low likelihood of college completion. And although African Americans are enrolled in postsecondary institutions at only a slightly lower rate than whites (34 percent compared with 38 percent) in Mississippi, the disparities in completion rates (39 percent compared with 54 percent at the baccalaureate level) suggest that postsecondary educational opportunity may be far from equitable based on race and other sociodemographic and economic indicators (*Measuring Up*, 2008).

A former HBCU president, Martin Jenkins (1958), quite accurately anticipated a lengthy and tedious desegregation process affected by various social and institutional challenges. Interestingly, he suggested that the desegregation of HBCUs will only increase in a "permissive social climate" (p. 419). He does not explicitly state that the fate of HBCUs and their desegregation efforts lies in the power of whites in terms of choosing to attend or work at HBCUs; however, it is alluded to: "as soon as an appreciable degree of desegregation occurs in a particular institution, questions of control, administration and continuing financial support will be raised" (p. 423). Jenkins's words would eventually come true, as both of West Virginia's HBCUs (Bluefield State and West Virginia State University) eventually came to have majority white student enrollments.

In terms of desegregation strategies, some scholars have provided tangible suggestions that HBCUs can use to satisfy the desegregation-integration issue (Baxter, 1982; Jenkins, 1958; Harley, 2001). In fact, two barriers to white integration at HBCUs are consistently noted: (1) the perceived poor academic quality of HBCUs and (2) whites' almost inevitable minority status on HBCU campuses as students, staff, or faculty (Harley, 2001). Some strategies suggested for recruiting whites to HBCUs include leveraging white students, alumni, faculty, and staff; establishing diversity training to promote inclusion;

evaluating campus climates; and developing scholarships, fellowships, and other programs specifically for white community building (Harley, Tennessee, Alston, and Wilson, 2000; Harley, 2001; Jenkins, 1958). Others suggest that a reexamination of the entire educational pipeline that abandons forced desegregation through assimilation and focuses on equitable resource allocation, racial and ethnic equality, and equal educational opportunity is necessary (Brady, Eatman, and Parker, 2000).

HBCUs continue to suffer from *de jure* segregation based on language, poor public policymaking, negative media attention, and sheer lack of power and resources (Gasman, 2008b; U.S. Department of Education, 2009b). As the notion of desegregating HBCUs continues even fifty years after *Brown*, the need to reflect on the philosophical underpinnings of equal educational opportunity is crucial. The fact that HBCUs have largely remained out of the national spotlight in terms of self-promotion may act to further isolate and engender onlookers' skepticism. In their legal fight for survival in the post-*Brown* and anti–affirmative action era, it is peculiar that HBCU advocates and leadership have remained relatively silent. Use of timely, theoretically justifiable, and empirically based claims as noted in Thomas and McPartland (1984) could prove useful, as the typical reliance on anecdotes seems insufficient.

In addition, the understandable lack of consensus among the African American community on HBCUs further complicates its role in a post-*Brown* era (Richardson and Harris, 2004). African Americans' migration outside the southern United States in conjunction with the expansion of the black middle class and student college choice, among other things, have certainly contributed to the complexity of black perceptions of HBCUs. Interestingly, the anti–affirmative action sentiment that began in the mid-1990s has apparently discouraged many African American (and other underrepresented) students from applying to HWIs and resulted in the reconsideration of HBCUs (Freeman and Thomas, 2002; McDonough, Antonio, and Trent, 1997; Tobolowsky, Outcalt, and McDonough, 2005). Although the affirmative action backlash is unfortunate, it ultimately supports HBCUs' ongoing assertion of providing equal educational opportunity for all students.

As judicial rulings directly affect publicly supported HBCUs, it is important to address the viability of private HBCUs, many of which continue to struggle. Jenkins (1958) wisely predicted that private HBCUs that persisted post-*Brown* would do so due as a result of increasingly selective admissions policies at historically white institutions and academic programmatic choices. Though legislation and court cases have affected public HBCU admissions criteria and African American enrollment, this premonition has proved accurate (Drewry and Doermann, 2001). In fact, *U.S. News & World Report*'s 2009 list of top HBCUs reveals that the top ten institutions are all part of the private sector. How and whether public HBCUs have been adversely affected by their private peers has yet to be examined, especially as HBCU enrollments overall have continued to rise.

Finally, the use of critical theory and its offshoots (such as critical race theory) to examine the role of HBCUs in American higher education appears beneficial for both practitioners and academicians. This perspective exposes inconsistencies in policy and policymaking that have adversely affected HBCUs, their students (regardless of race), and the American quest for equal educational opportunity.

Over the years, the American judicial system has wavered in its commitment to HBCUs, confusing issues of justice, equity, equality, and race-blind policies (M. C. Brown, 2001). This lack of commitment is evidenced by the court's inability to explicitly uphold HBCUs in the context of both desegregation and integration. For HBCU proponents, the past notion of white integration at HBCUs and black desegregation of HWIs as the only viable solution to equal educational opportunity for African Americans and other underrepresented groups is truly outdated (M. C. Brown, 2001).

Students

B Y AND LARGE, THE BULK OF THE RESEARCH on HBCUs pertains to their students. In general, the research on HBCU students has been used to describe African American undergraduate demographic and academic characteristics. Over the years, this research evolved to incorporate comparisons between African American students attending HBCUs and those attending HWIs as well as their labor market outcomes. More recently, however, the research on HBCU students, though still primarily focused on descriptions of undergraduates, has become more robust to reflect the higher educational research canon, including studies of college choice, socialization, health, identity development, and gender.

Since the mid-1970s, seminal works by numerous scholars have focused on comparative research to gauge HBCU and HWI students focusing on multiple aspects of higher education. For example, some studies examine college choice (Conrad, Brier, and Braxton, 1997; Freeman, 1999, 2005; Freeman and Thomas, 2002; McDonough, Antonio, and Trent, 1997; Tobolowsky, Outcalt, and McDonough, 2005), campus experiences (Boone, 2003; Harvey and Williams, 1989; Kim, 2002; Kimbrough, Molock, and Walton, 1996; Outcalt and Skewes-Cox, 2002), achievement (DeSousa and Kuh, 1996; Kim, 2002; Kim and Conrad, 2006; Nasim, Roberts, Harrell, and Young, 2005), persistence (Wilson, 2007), identity (Berger and Milem, 2000; Cokley, 2005; Lott, 2008; Wade, 2002), and outcomes (Allen, 1992; Berger and Milem; 2000; Constantine, 1995; Dreher and Chargois, 1998; Flowers, 2002; Kim, 2002; Perna, 2001; Sibulkin and Butler, 2005; Strayhorn, 2008).

Although the literature on HBCU students is vast, in general contextualization in terms of the institution and changes in the student body over time are lacking. In addition, very little research has been done on graduate and professional students (Garrett, 2006; Hall and Closson, 2005; Ladson, Lin, Flores, and Magrane, 2006) and on nonblack students. As scholars have made great strides to improve the HBCU canon, expansion in some unexpected areas has occurred as well. In fact, the number of epidemiological and health-related articles that pertain to HBCU students and address gender has increased (see, for example, Chung and Carlon, 2006; Laws and others, 2006; Laws, Holliday, and Huang, 2007; Gabbidon and others, 2008; Thompson-Robins and others, 2005; Valentine, Wright, and Henley, 2003; Wagner, Liles, Broadnax, and Nuriddin-Little, 2006). Unfortunately, this research has not been well incorporated into the higher education HBCU student research just yet. Implicit in all the HBCU student research are notions of diversity, gender, and identity. Furthermore, the legacy of HBCU success also implies consideration of the HBCU environment and student outcomes.

College Choice

Understandably, the lack of research on HBCU college choice and their largely African American student populations was virtually unnecessary until the mid-twentieth century, as HBCUs served as the primary postsecondary education access point for black students. During the post-*Brown* era, focus increased on black students at HBCUs and HWIs, yet this research often focused on students' experiences, while a small few focused on college choice. The research on HBCU college choice has expanded for at least two reasons, however.

First, this research addressed African American students explicitly (McDonough, Antonio, and Trent, 1997), as most four-year HBCUs had (and continue to have) black enrollments well above 85 percent (U.S. Department of Education, 2009a; Provasnik, Shafer, and Snyder, 2004). In addition, the higher education research on college choice in general rarely focused specifically on African American students. Second, in the post-*Brown* era where college choice has expanded for all groups, it has become important to use college choice research to explain why students choose HBCUs and incorporate that into rationales for continuing support for these institutions (Conrad, Brier, and Braxton, 1997; Freeman, 1999; Tobolowsky, Outcalt, and McDonough, 2005). Another issue that HBCU college choice research appears to address is student recruitment and retention strategies, for both black and nonblack students.

The body of literature on choice of HBCU essentially built on research comparing black student experiences on HBCU and HWI campuses (Allen, 1992; Fleming, 1984; Gurin and Epps, 1975). Although the seminal works of the mid- to late-twentieth century identified demographic and academic differences in African American matriculants at HBCUs and HWIs, they failed to provide a comprehensive understanding of students considering and subsequently enrolling in HBCUs. This void is arguably justified, however. Unlike many of the larger, typically quantitative studies of college choice that are supported by survey data such as the National Assessment of Educational Progress and the National Education Longitudinal Studies, few survey samples include a significant number of African American HBCU students (Perna, 2001). As a result, the research on HBCU college choice is largely framed by qualitative research.

An important first step in understanding African American HBCU college choice involves college-bound high school students. In a five-city (Atlanta, New York, Washington, D.C., Chicago, and Los Angeles) multischool study using sixteen structured group interviews, Freeman (1999) interviewed seventy tenth-, eleventh-, and twelfth-grade African American students. Focusing her efforts on large urban cities and using purposive sampling in private schools, Freeman identified three factors contributing to the consideration of HBCUs during the college process: personal affiliation, appreciation of the HBCU legacy, and interest in the HBCU majority-black environment (Freeman, 1999). Although often cited to provide a basis from which to understand black college choice, this research has important limitations, namely the unsystematic sampling. An additional limitation pertains to the failure to identify students' post–high school matriculation. Although the conclusions from this study were informative, the model is essentially unconfirmed because there is no consideration of students' subsequent postsecondary choices. Further, a considerable amount of data and research suggests that large proportions of African American students at HBCUs have come from predominately black educational and social environments (U.S. Department of Education, 2009a), while this study focused specifically on black students from secondary schools with large white populations.

Building on the research on high school students, McDonough, Antonio, and Trent (1997) considered how race, ethnicity, and class affect freshmen students' access and social mobility. Data from the UCLA Cooperative Institutional Research Program's 1993 freshman survey identified a sample of approximately thirty institutions and two hundred thousand full-time, first-time students for the regression analysis. The descriptive analysis revealed that HBCU students hailed from families with incomes less than $20,000 and had lower academic achievement records than African American students at HWIs (McDonough, Antonio, and Trent, 1997). In terms of college choice, these students also picked HBCUs largely because of personal affiliations—that is, they knew someone who attended one of these institutions, a finding similar to Freeman's work (1999). Descriptive statistics also indicated that many African American students at both HBCUs and HWIs were influenced by geography, living in or near an HBCU state. With such proximity, it is not surprising that students who matriculated to HBCUs often had an encouraging personal affiliation.

In their brief literature review on the characteristics of students who consider HBCUs, Freeman and Thomas (2002) note both student and institutional characteristics as important in college choice. Financial resources appear to play a significant role in African American college choice in general, and especially in HBCU choice (Cross and Astin, 1981; Hossler and Gallagher, 1987). This finding coincides precisely with HBCUs' well-documented commitment to low tuition charges and enrollment of a largely low-income student body (for example, the White House Initiative on HBCUs places the level of low-income HBCU students at 70 percent [U.S. Department of Education, 2009a]) and students with low to moderate academic competitiveness (U.S. Department of Education, 2009a; Hossler and Gallagher, 1987).

An important consideration related to research on HBCU student college choice pertains to the nonblack population. In one of the more well-cited articles, Conrad, Brier, and Braxton (1997) conducted research on white HBCU students to assess the "desegregation" of HBCUs. Interestingly, the authors enlisted white students, faculty, and staff and found that the primary reasons for white student matriculation at HBCUs included financial aid, academic programs, and institutional characteristics (Conrad, Brier, and Braxton, 1997). This study's research design is confusing, however, for two reasons. First, the contributions of faculty and staff as a way to inform college choice are not typically used in college choice research. Second, the authors gloss over the fact that some white HBCU students made their decisions because of financial need or because they were less academically competitive as their same-race peers at nearby HWIs (Conrad, Brier, and Braxton, 1997).

Although the small and growing body of literature on HBCU college choice is important, two important limitations remain. First, the number of four-year HBCUs has consistently remained at 105 or fewer institutions, representing generally 3 percent of American postsecondary institutions. Although this reality is not debilitating for HBCU college choice as a research topic, it contributes to the institutions' and their students' absence in many studies, especially national surveys. As such, few studies of HBCU college choice are sufficiently cross-sectional, and thus stakeholders are relegated to a body of research that is limited methodologically and may be outdated.

Second, many HBCUs have considerable undergraduate populations consisting of foreign nationals as well as other American racial and ethnic groups (Hill, 1984; U.S. Department of Education, 2009a; Willie, 1994). As such, HBCU college choice research ought to incorporate these underrepresented populations, particularly in the wake of post-*Brown* efforts to "desegregate" or increase the nonblack student population. It may also be important to consider how college counselors are familiar with HBCUs and how that affects students' decisions about college (Tobolowsky, Outcalt, and McDonough, 2005). Finally, as HBCUs continue to counter attacks on their continued presence among the American higher education landscape, theoretically sound and empirically based social science research on HBCU college choice can provide the necessary evidence of their viability, efficiency, and success, regardless of methodological approach.

Gender

The literature on African American students at HBCUs is quite ambiguous in relation to gender. On the one hand, it contains multiple assertions that

HBCUs are the most viable institutions for all African American students (Allen, 1992; Brown and Freeman, 2004; Fleming, 1984; Williams and Ashley, 2004; Willie, Reddick, and Brown, 2006). On the other hand, the reality of relatively poor achievement, enrollment, and undergraduate degree completion by African American males at HBCUs suggests a gendered effect (Geiger, 2007; U.S. Department of Education, 2009a; Nettles and Perna, 1997; Provasnik, Shafer, and Snyder, 2004). In some comparison studies, particularly those where aggregate institutional or racial and ethnic group data are used, gender is often not mentioned (for example, Ehrenberg and Rothstein, 1994; Kim, 2002; Kimbrough, Molock, and Walton, 1996; Outcalt and Skewes-Cox, 2002). Nonetheless, a respectable body of literature on gender at HBCUs is available, even if it does appear to afford more attention to women than men.

Often literature on HBCU students is used to clarify or justify, either implicitly or explicitly, the existence of the venerable institutions (see, for example, American Association of University Professors, 1995; Allen and Jewell, 2002; Bowles and DeCosta, 1971; M. C. Brown, 1999; Brown, Donahoo, and Bertrand, 2001; Harvey and Williams, 1989; Jaffe, Adams, and Meyers, 1968; Willie and Edmonds, 1978). As a result, reference to gender is not typically highlighted, as aggregate data on black students have been sufficient to document HBCU successes in terms of enrollment and completion.

Examinations of gender at HBCUs often refer to one of the most seminal texts on the subject, Fleming's *Blacks in College* (1984), which attempts to assess whether HBCUs or HWIs better develop African American college students. Interestingly, the book compares white students at HWIs and therefore analyzes data on both black and white men and women at HWIs and black men and women at HBCUs. Drawing on cross-sectional data from multiple institutions, the author points out important differences between African American students attending HBCUs. For example, the research echoes findings by multiple scholars indicating that African American women experience marginalization on HBCU campuses both inside and outside the classroom (see, for example, Allen and Haniff, 1991; Bonner, 2001; Geiger, 2007; Gurin and Epps, 1975). In general, the research suggests African American women at HBCUs are more likely to feel dominated in the classroom and in extracurricular activities, are less likely to engage with faculty members, and often choose academic majors that fit gender stereotypes (Allen, 1992; Fleming, 1984; Bonner, 2001). Interestingly, most larger studies of gender at HBCUs were conducted before the mid-1990s, and thus the nature of these gender-related experiences at HBCUs appears to be changing. For example, some have suggested that African American women have made significant strides in terms of improving their engagement and achievement. Harper, Carini, Bridges, and Hayek (2004) reveal that African American women are more engaged with the HBCU community, taking more leadership roles, interacting with faculty more frequently, and thus feeling less isolated than their same-race male peers. In addition, HBCUs play a significant role in promoting science, technology, engineering, and mathematics (STEM) careers for African American women (Solorzano, 1995), as noted in studies of STEM doctoral recipients and a more recent study of Spelman College. Although this research focused on one single-sex institution, the research identified another all-women's HBCU (Bennett College) and coeducational HBCUs that contribute more than 15 percent of STEM bachelor's degree for African American women annually, even though HBCUs represent only 3 percent of postsecondary institutions (Perna and others, 2009).

With regard to African American men at HBCUs and their experiences, the seminal works focus largely on their dominance of the campus, inside and outside the classroom. In fact, after noting that African American men were "dominant" on HBCU campuses, Fleming (1984) describes a perplexing interpersonal "aloofness" that she never revisited in her book: "In the supportive environments of black colleges, where Black men feel accepted, interpersonal issues become almost irrelevant to them. They show far less concern for others. They use the many opportunities for comforting relationships to reach a state of interpersonal detachment. Thus, in a warm environment where there are many opportunities for relatedness, black males strive to remain unaffected by people" (p. 143). In sum, although Fleming (1984) considers both gender and race in the research design and analysis, a noticeable disparity exists in the attention afforded African American male and female student issues. In fact, seemingly contradictory findings about the black male experience are highlighted, though never explicitly questioned or explored. In the end, this work easily concludes that HBCUs better develop African American students than

HWIs, providing little to no qualification of black male experiences at HBCUs. Interestingly, this research is quite representative of the research on gender at HBCUs.

A subset of HBCU literature explores the role of gender in these environments (see Bonner, 2001; Cokley, 2001; Gasman, 2007b; Geiger, 2007; Harper, Carini, Bridges, and Hayek, 2004; Peters and others, 2005; Tabbye and others, 2004; Wang, Browne, Storr, and Wagner, 2005). In fact, although some documents provide descriptive statistics on gender at HBCUs with little analysis of the disparity (see, for example, Geiger, 2007; Nettles and Perna, 1997; Nettles, Perna, Edelin, and Robertson, 1996; Provasnik, Shafer, and Snyder, 2004), some empirically based publications explicitly consider gender at HBCUs. Interestingly, this literature is often titled without a specific focus on men or women in the research design, thereby implying consideration of both gender groups (for example, Allen and Haniff, 1991; Bonner, 2001; Cokley, 2001; Harper, Carini, Bridges, and Hayek, 2004; Watt, 2006).

In-depth review of these gender-focused works, however, suggests that issues related to gender at HBCUs are often a reference to women, as few studies afford a critical lens on African American males. For example, Harper, Carini, Bridges, and Hayek (2004) examined student engagement and satisfaction gender gaps at HBCUs. After noting the underrepresentation of African American men in the research design, the results revealed no significant gender differences on six of the eight measures of engagement. The findings were eventually summarized as "HBCU women no longer lag behind men in their academic and social engagement experiences" (p. 277), noting that African American male dominance has "subsided considerably" (p. 280). Interestingly, this presentation of research appears to put side by side the gains of black women and the losses of black men, though not necessarily intentionally. Furthermore, although the authors thoughtfully questioned why seemingly engaged African American men at HBCUs have relatively low persistence rates, the discussion and implications were primarily focused on women (Harper, Carini, Bridges, and Hayek, 2004).

Interestingly, extra attention to women at HBCUs seems indicative of other HBCU gender research as well. Bonner (2001) attempts to inspire dialogue on gender at HBCUs; however, a review of the research questions reveals black women are the focal point. In addition, Gasman's historiography of gender and black colleges (2007b) effectively reviews and critiques the systematic exclusion of African American women in HBCU history, leadership, and longevity. Although the review sheds light on black male-dominated administration of HBCUs, it does little to consider African American male students (Gasman, 2007b). In effect, a steadily growing body of literature on gender at HBCUs essentially highlights the African American female experience (for example, Bonner, 2001; Ferguson, Quinn, Eng, and Sandelowski, 2006; Gasman, 2007b; Lent and others, 2005; Watt, 2006).

Other publications on gender at HBCUs provide a more balanced analysis, pointing out the obstacles facing both male and female students. For example, Chavous and others (2004) examine racial stereotype expectations, gender, academic self-concept, and academic performance of African American students at an HBCU and an HWI. The findings note the complexities of race, gender, and academic major in the HBCU environment (Chavous and others, 2004). Moreover, although the authors connect their results to others' work, noting black women's marginalization at HBCUs, they explicitly admit their research design does not permit determination of "how or whether African American men are experiencing different types of responses and reactions from their college institution than are African American women" (Chavous and others, 2004, p. 13). Supporting this more balanced consideration of gender at HBCUs, some scholars have also noted the fallacy of assuming that African American students at HBCUs do not face socially constructed or derived barriers (related to gender, economics, or race, for example) (Kimbrough and Harper, 2006).

African American Males

Although research that broadly focuses on gender and HBCUs falls short in providing men and women equal attention, a small and growing body of literature specifically examines African American men (see, for example, Kimbrough and Harper, 2006; Palmer and Gasman, 2008; Palmer and Strayhorn, 2008; Riggins, McNeal, and Herndon, 2008; M. J. Ross, 1998). Much in the same spirit of comparison studies, some of this research provides an empirically based justification for HBCUs' continued existence by highlighting the successes of African American male students (Palmer and Gasman, 2008; Riggins, McNeal, and Herndon, 2008; M. J. Ross, 1998). Along these lines, the single-institution case studies by Palmer and colleagues (see Palmer and Gasman, 2008; Palmer and Strayhorn, 2008) provide in-depth consideration of the benefits African American men receive on HBCU campuses. In one study, eleven graduating black male students at one institution were interviewed to discuss their success, despite having been academically underprepared when they entered college (Palmer and Gasman, 2008). Confirming others' findings, the authors identify a common theme around participants' responses, specifically the nurturing and supportive environment (the institution, its students, staff, and faculty) that enabled study participants to develop social capital that both inspired and propelled their postsecondary success (Palmer and Gasman, 2008).

Along other lines, Kimbrough and Harper (2006) provide an informative, though preliminary, consideration of the barriers that African American male students face on HBCU campuses. In fact, in the beginning of their piece, the authors note the gender gaps in HBCU enrollment, persistence, and completion and then challenge the assumption "that PWIs are mainly responsible for the low retention and degree completion rates of racial and ethnic minority college students"—or black male students in this case (Kimbrough and Harper, 2006, p. 191). In addition to providing a critical analysis of descriptive statistics, Kimbrough and Harper (2006) present the findings of in-depth focus groups with African American male student leaders from multiple HBCUs, focusing on both their personal experiences and perceptions of black men at HBCUs overall. Reminiscent of the "aloofness" Fleming (1984) used to describe black men, the participants in Kimbrough and Harper's study (2006) indicated that African American men at HBCUs experienced barriers related to interpersonal relationship building. Not only were those relationships between black male and female peers noted, but relationships with family and on-campus institutional supports (counselors, faculty, and staff) were also mentioned. All were perceived to negatively contribute to their same-race, same-gender peers' lack of success.

African American Females

As black women have historically constituted a majority of the black undergraduate population at HBCUs (Hill, 1984; Geiger 2007; Nettles and Perna, 1997; Provasnik, Shafer, and Snyder, 2004), it is surprising that such a relatively small body of literature focuses exclusively on these students, their experiences, and outcomes. One important note pertains to African American women's dispersion through the degree levels at HBCUs. Although descriptive data reveal that African American women have nearly always constituted a larger proportion of the HBCU undergraduate population, their presence has been less prevalent in graduate and professional academic programs (U.S. Department of Education, 2009a; Provasnik, Shafer, and Snyder, 2004), an area of research that is vastly underexamined.

Although African American women may be prevalent on HBCU campuses, that fact has not negated the male-dominated American value system (Bonner, 2001; Gasman 2007b). In fact, evidence suggests that compared with their same-race and same-gender peers at coeducational HBCUs, single-sex HBCUs (such as Bennett and Spelman Colleges) are more sensitive and conducive to African American women's identity development (Bonner, 2001; Watt, 2006). This research supports the findings of comparison studies on gender at HBCUs that note African American women as isolated, socially docile, and less likely to engage with their mostly male faculty and administrators.

Because relatively few empirical studies of HBCU students exist in comparison with students overall, it is not surprising that the research on student gender at HBCUs is not definitive. Although the comparative studies explicitly set out to examine gender differences at HBCUs, the experiences of each gender are considered with what appears to be a notable focus on women. This reality is not surprising, as the black woman's role has been transformed as a result of societal changes affecting both women and African Americans. Coincidentally, these changes have probably led to the lack of attention—both practically and theoretically—to African American men on HBCU campuses. The changing context of HBCUs and American society necessitates additional research on gender at HBCUs to contextualize more accurately marginalization, successes, and challenges.

Campus Environments

Proponents often anecdotally hail HBCUs as some of the best institutions for African Americans because of their nurturing environments. Interestingly, few scholars have made the characterization of the HBCU college environment a primary focal point. In some cases, scholars have provided well-evidenced justifications for how HBCUs have propelled black students through postsecondary success, noting relatively smaller classes; faculty advising; a built-in support system from African American peers, faculty, and administrators; and access to formal remedial programs (DeSousa and Kuh, 1996; Flowers, 2002).

Just after the *Brown* ruling, it was important for scholars and practitioners to conduct research on college campus environments to help gauge the process of postsecondary desegregation. In fact, the majority of research on the HBCU environment was developed through comparative studies of African American students at HBCUs and HWIs (Berger and Milem, 2000; Fleming, 1984; Flowers, 2002; Farazzo and Stevens, 2004; Kim, 2002; Nasim, Roberts, Harrell, and Young, 2005; Outcalt and Skewes-Cox, 2002). In some cases, this comparison research was used to point out the hostility African American students experienced on HWI campuses and the more welcoming environment at HBCUs (Fleming, 1984). This largely cross-sectional research suggests that African American students at HBCUs are more satisfied and academically engaged than their same-race peers on HWI campuses (Allen, 1992; Bonous-Hammarth and Boatsman, 1996; Fleming, 1984; Fries-Britt and Turner, 2002; Outcalt and Skewes-Cox, 2002). That is, these students ask questions in class, interact with faculty and staff more, and are more likely to participate in extracurricular activities (Boone, 2003; Chism and Satcher, 1998; DeSousa and Kuh, 1996; Flowers, 2002; Kim, 2002). In addition, considerable attention has been paid to the role of social organizations in providing African American students at HBCUs with outlets for engagement (Brown, Parks, and Phillips, 2005; Kimbrough, 2003; L. Ross, 2001; Turner-Musa and Wilson, 2006). Though the research does not explicitly connect the effect of the HBCU environment to African American student achievement, many scholars imply that these factors as interrelated (Allen and Haniff, 1991; DeSousa and Kuh, 1996; Nasim, Roberts, Harrell, and Young, 2005).

Although considerable research suggests that the HBCU environment is better for African American students, it is important to qualify this generalization, as Kimbrough, Molock, and Walton (1996) cautioned: "One cannot assume that African American students at predominately Black universities are necessarily better off" (p. 305). In addition, much of this research is based on a social context just after integration was legalized and should be considered appropriately in more contemporary work. Finally, it is important to note that with few exceptions (for example, Blake, 2006; Closson and Henry, 2008; Conrad, Brier, and Braxton, 1997; Nixon and Henry, 1992) characterizations of HBCU students focus on African American students only. As more non-black students begin to enroll in HBCUs, it may be important to consider their presence in research on the HBCU environment and whether it is indeed as nurturing for them as it appears to be for African American students. Last, as HBCUs become more comfortable with the topic of homosexuality and the presence of openly gay students, it will be important for researchers to examine the experiences of those gay and lesbian students who attend black colleges.

Graduation and Outcomes

Although the anecdotal and empirical research indicates that the HBCU environment plays a significant role in outcomes for African American students, the focus of such research lies in multiple areas. In addition to considering persistence and graduation rates for HBCU students, important data are available on graduate matriculation, doctoral degree receipt, and labor market outcomes.

First, research on postsecondary outcomes often focuses on economic gains, coinciding with the notion of education as "the great equalizer" (Allen, 1992; Constantine, 1995; Ehrenberg and Rothstein, 1994; Fryer and Greenston, 2007; Strayhorn, 2008). Like other HBCU research, this body is ladled with comparative work on HBCUs and HWIs. Interestingly, the findings do not consistently show that attending an HBCU is better or worse. Strayhorn (2008) attempts to reconcile this literature by examining differences in salary, occupational status, and job satisfaction using a national dataset for a cohort of bachelor's degree recipients from 1993. The findings suggest that attending an

HBCU may be detrimental to labor market outcomes (Strayhorn, 2008). Although this research was an improvement over past research methodologically and conceptually, it is cross-sectional and thus is relevant for only a snapshot in time (see Webster, Stockard, and Henson, 1981, or Wilson, 2007). This type of economically based research incorporates societal changes, and because such changes wax and wane over time, this area of research ought to remain at the forefront of scholars' agendas.

With the increase in calls for accountability in higher education has come more attention to persistence and graduation rates at HBCUs (Allen, 1992; Kim and Conrad, 2006; Nettles and Perna, 1997; Wilson, 2007). The research on African American persistence at HBCUs appears to indicate that, compared with HWIs, students who enroll in HBCUs as first-time, full-time students are more likely to eventually obtain a bachelor's degree (Allen, 1992; Ehrenberg and Rothstein, 1994). Some research, however, contradicts this statement or suggests that students attending either type of institution are just as likely to receive a degree (DeSousa and Kuh, 1996; Kim, 2002; Kim and Conrad, 2006; Wilson, 2007). For proponents of HBCUs, all these findings support claims that HWIs could improve their role in promoting African American access, persistence, and degree completion, as they have historically held more human and financial resources compared with HBCUs (see Brady, Eatman, and Parker, 2000). In the same vein, this research bolsters proponents' claims to justify the maintenance and continued support of HBCUs.

Some of the most interesting research on African American HBCU student outcomes relates to the lack of reliance on traditional cognitive measures such as grade point average to predict achievement. Although academic ability is often characterized as a primary independent variable in research on postsecondary outcomes, multiple scholars attribute noncognitive factors to achievement at HBCUs. For example, in studies of psychosocial student attributes, some have found that the HBCU cultural context promotes racial identity development that positively affects academic achievement (Allen, 1992; DeSousa and Kuh, 1996; Nasim, Roberts, Harrell, and Young, 2005).

Along other lines, some research suggests that African American matriculation to an HBCU may not be so positive (see, for example, Lang, 1986). Descriptive data posted by the Education Trust in 2009 indicate that graduation rates for

African American students at HBCUs are relatively low. This finding is especially detrimental to HBCUs as they face the post-*Fordice* and anti–affirmative action climate that often interprets the resource-limited HBCUs' challenges in graduating (African American) students as a need for institutional merger or closure. Some attempts have been successful, however, to identify, modify, implement, and reproduce programs that support retention efforts at HBCUs (Hale, 2006; Nettles, Wagener, Millett, and Killenbeck, 1999).

Besides research on the disproportionate role HBCUs play in producing African American undergraduate and graduate degree holders (Solorzano, 1995; U.S. Department of Education, 2009a), more research is needed on HBCU students, especially research that addresses the social and historical context. First, with regard to labor market outcomes, little research is available that considers the role the institutional sector plays on individual graduates or local and national economies. Second, the research on HBCU student outcomes focuses on African American students. Because the nonblack community is growing at many HBCUs (U.S. Department of Education, 2009a), interesting and important information is yet to be explored fully in HBCUs' nonblack student body. Finally, consistent data collection and analysis of HBCU student records must be maintained and publicly available (U.S. Department of Education, 2009a) for both students and institutions; without a robust dataset, correlations and predictive modeling of HBCU students and their outcomes cannot be identified or, more important, replicated at other HBCUs and HWIs. This line of research might prove beneficial in identifying a more substantive link between HBCUs' nurturing environment and students' success (or challenges).

Presidential Leadership

L EADERSHIP AT HBCUs is a current and vital topic in higher education. It is also a source of controversy. Outside critics as well as those in
the HBCU arena complain about "recycled" presidents, authoritarian leadership, lack of shared governance, and trampled academic freedom. On the other
hand, certain exemplary leaders choose skilled academic administrators and
talented faculty members, letting them do their jobs and rarely interfering
unless a major crisis occurs. Despite myriad biographies and autobiographies
of HBCU presidents and coverage of their lives in institutional histories, more
can be learned about these individuals (Benjamin, 2004; M. C. Brown, 1998;
Carter, 1998; Davis, 1998; Engs, 1999; Gasman, 1999, 2001a, 2001b, 2001c;
Gilpin and Gasman, 2003; Goodson, 1991; Manley, 1995; Mays, 2003;
McKinney, 1997; Nichols, 2004; Robbins, 1996; G. Smith, 1994; Urban,
1994; Watson and Gregory, 2005; Williamson, 2004b). Racism and Jim Crow
mentalities made it incredibly difficult for HBCU leaders to perform their duties,
protect their students, and maintain the integrity of their campuses. Moreover,
as HBCU presidents contend with the looming questions of why HBCUs
should exist in a post-*Brown* America (and now "postracial" America in the age
of Barack Obama), their perspectives and commentary are even more vital.

Diverse in tone and content, depictions of black college presidents have
been crafted by myriad supporters and critics over the past seventy-five years.
As leadership of black colleges began to shift from white to black hands in the
early part of the twentieth century, some African Americans came to
the defense of black college presidents against the doubts of white skeptics.
Carter G. Woodson (1933), for example, lashed out against lack of white

confidence in black college leadership: "It is often said, too, that the time is not ripe for Negroes to take over the administration of their institutions, for they do not have the contacts for raising money; but what becomes of this argument when we remember what Booker T. Washington did for Tuskegee and observe what R. R. Moton and John Hope are doing today?" (p. 30). Although Woodson supported black leadership at black colleges, others were much more critical. Gunnar Myrdal, the Swedish sociologist, discussed black college leadership in his book *An American Dilemma,* arguing that black college leaders acquired a "dictatorial and paternalistic" demeanor toward blacks and imitated the leadership style of white southerners (1944, pp. 732–733).

In his now classic *Black Bourgeoisie,* E. Franklin Frazier wrote a scornful portrayal of the black middle class, arguing that black college leaders were key to the problems of the African American middle class. In particular, Frazier noted, "The segregated schools in which Negro teachers had to find employment were generally under the autocratic control of Negroes chosen by the Whites who gave financial support to the schools. . . . [It] amounted to what is known in the field of colonial administrations as a system of 'indirect rule'" (Frazier, 1957, p. 97).

In 1967, Harvard professors Christopher Jencks and David Riesman labeled black colleges "academic disaster areas." Throughout their article their depictions of black colleges and their leaders are overwhelmingly negative; they describe the black college presidents as "frightened" and accuse them of "tyrannizing" the faculty (p. 22).

Writing in 1973, sociologist and black college faculty member Daniel C. Thompson included an extensive, more even-handed, discussion of black college presidents in his book *Private Black Colleges at the Crossroads,* examining their leadership through the early 1970s. Specifically, he claimed, "Black college presidents are, on the whole, extremely capable people who would rank very high on any scale of administrative ability, and should have no need to be afraid of subordinate administrators" (p. 242).

In 1978, Charles Willie and Raymond Edmonds challenged Jencks and Riesman's attack on black college presidents, noting that "Christopher Jencks and David Riesman . . . have charged that many black colleges are run 'as if they were the personal property of their presidents'" (p. 133). Willie and

Edmonds allowed that presidents of black colleges have asserted sometimes unnecessary control but not, in their opinion, for selfish reasons: "Black-college presidents have remained visibly in control. But their control has been for the sake of preserving their institutions" (p. 133).

Some attempts have been made in recent years to study the black college presidency, but they have not been comprehensive in nature. These attempts have consisted of compilations of presidents' perspectives on leadership or interviews with presidents (Mbajekwe, 2006; Ricard and Brown, 2008). Mbajekwe (2006), for example, edited a volume that includes the perspectives of ten HBCU presidents from a diverse cross-section of the institutional community. In addition to recounting the historic role that HBCUs have played in American higher education, the presidents contemplate the current mission of these institutions and the influence of diversity on this mission. Of note as well, the HBCU presidents discuss the fundraising challenges that they face as leaders and that their institutions face as a result of the historical legacy of racism. Unfortunately, Mbajekwe provides little analysis of the presidents' perspectives except in the introduction to her book.

Ricard and Brown (2008) recently authored *Ebony Towers in Higher Education,* a book that aims to increase our understanding of the mission and leadership of HBCUs. Their book gives an overview of HBCUs, offers profiles of selected black colleges and their presidents and discusses the unique mission of these institutions. The difficulty with this book is that the HBCUs featured in the book are assigned pseudonyms, and, as a result, the reader does not learn much about specific HBCUs. In effect, the pseudonyms prevent the reader from understanding the particularities of each institution's circumstance. In addition, the book includes quotes from the HBCU presidents who were interviewed for the book but very little analysis of these quotes. That said, the quotes are revealing, engaging, and could be wonderfully useful with additional critical reflection. For example, the HBCU presidents discuss their views on students, strategic planning, preparation for the position, and the uniqueness of HBCUs. Of note, throughout the book are many quotes from HBCU presidents that speak to issues of control. Even those presidents who talked about having a collaborative leadership style used language such as "the buck stops here" or "I'm involved in everything that happens at this institution."

Given that this critique of HBCU presidents is salient, the authors should have taken on the issue of control and interrogated it. What are the ramifications of a controlling president? Why does the president feel the need to control most aspects of the campus? Where did he or she learn this behavior? Do we see the same behaviors among leaders of HWIs? Overall, we know very little about the leadership of HBCUs, and what we do know is focused on male leadership with a few exceptions (for example, Willa Player and Mary McLeod Bethune) and is historical in nature.

Given the stereotypes and generalizations made about HBCU leaders as well as the future of these institutions—which hangs in the balance—it is essential that new scholars interrogate the leadership styles and decision making of HBCU presidents, perhaps with a focus on women. In addition, as demonstrated, most of the literature related to HBCU presidents is negative in tone; scholars should aim to examine the lives and actions of a more diverse set of presidents, with the goal of providing a more comprehensive and nuanced depiction of these individuals.

Faculty and Governance Issues

FACULTY AT TWO- AND FOUR-YEAR HBCUs comprise more than fifty thousand individuals. Although HBCU faculty represent only a small portion of postsecondary teaching staff in the country, the achievements of HBCUs in terms of African American student success throughout history make the lack of information on their faculty peculiar. In general, the literature—both academic and popular—focuses largely on faculty governance, socialization, and diversity (that is, the nonblack teaching staff). Although these issues are important, they shed light on only part of the historical and contextual description and experience of HBCU faculty.

Faculty Diversity

Faculty diversity at HBCUs is often considered distinct from that of historically white institutions because of the sizable proportion of nonblack teaching faculty but also because of the critical mass of African American academicians (Foster, Guyden, and Miller, 1999). In fact, data from the 2001 Integrated Postsecondary Education Data System surveys suggest that 72 percent of HBCU full-time faculty were African American, Latina, Latino, Native American, or Asian/Pacific Islander; whites accounted for 27 percent of full-time HBCU faculty during that same year (Provasnik, Shafer, and Snyder, 2004).

White participation among HBCU faculty is directly related to the origins and social impetus for black education in the United States (Anderson, 1988; Gasman, 2008a). During the late nineteenth and early twentieth centuries, white philanthropy virtually guaranteed white participation in all aspects of black institutions in terms of planning, mission, structure, and employment patterns (Foster, Guyden, and Miller, 1999; Gasman, 2008a; Jewell, 2002). Though the presence of white faculty members at HBCUs has varied across individual institutions and with time, whites have been a noticeable presence on HBCU campuses as far back as the mid-1920s (Anderson, 1988). The presence of white faculty members at HBCUs was especially prominent between the 1940s and 1950s, when whites, especially Jewish scholars, escaped persecution and were provided academic refuge at many HBCUs (Edgecomb, 1993; Meier, 1992).

In general, the presence of white faculty members during this era was seen as a necessary evil, a position that gained significant support during the civil rights movement. African Americans, including those at HBCUs, began to publicly question the presence of whites among the HBCU faculty and administration (Williamson, 2008). This position of caution and skepticism at HBCUs has not only persisted but also resulted in a considerable body of literature on white faculty and their experiences at HBCUs (see, for example, Cooper, Massey and Graham, 2006; Foster, 2001; Foster, Guyden, and Miller, 1999; Meier, 1992; Smith and Borgstedt, 1985).

Much of the large percentage of African Americans among HBCU faculty compared with HWI faculty can be attributed to the nature of HBCUs themselves. In fact, HBCUs produce a significant number of African American faculty members (Provasnik, Shafer, and Snyder, 2004), especially those in the fields of education, science, mathematics, and engineering (Perna, 2001; Solorzano, 1995). For example, more than half the full-time African American faculty members with bachelor's degrees from HBCUs are employed at HBCUs (Perna, 2001). In addition, among African Americans having earned their doctoral degrees at HBCUs, approximately 70 percent work at HBCUs (Perna, 2001).

With regard to gender diversity among faculty, women represented approximately 42 percent of HBCU full-time faculty members in 2001 (Provasnik, Shafer, and Snyder, 2004). Interestingly, when institutional type is considered, women account for a small majority (54.1 percent) among faculty in two-year HBCUs (Provasnik, Shafer, and Snyder, 2004).

Although a sizable body of research is available on faculty diversity in general (see, for example, Milem and Astin, 1993; Singh, Robinson, and Williams-Green, 1995), it often excludes HBCU faculty. Although considerable attention is paid to race, ethnicity, and gender among the faculty at HBCUs, research considering more nuanced differences (or similarities) based on institutional sector, full- or part-time status, individuals working at two- or four-year institutions, and those on and off the tenure track is quite limited.

Critique of Governance

HBCUs are often scrutinized and criticized because of their lack of formal governance structures, especially when compared with HWIs (Billingsley, 1982; Guy-Sheftall, 2006; Phillips, 2002). According to Guy-Sheftall (2006), faculty members at HBCUs have historically played a noncritical role in activities like changing the curriculum, appointment of academic leaders (including provosts and department chairs), or capital campaigns. In fact, shared governance at HBCUs is often characterized as a tangible source of tension between faculty and administrators, where the latter are constrained by the history and tradition of HBCUs and under pressure in some cases, leading to isolation and ostracism of outspoken faculty members (Minor, 2005).

Although these critiques shed light on important aspects of faculty life at HBCUs that are distinctly different at HWIs in general, they often neglect to account for the HBCU context. For example, in describing how to build a strong black HBCU faculty, Billingsley (1982) revisits the HBCU focus on service and effectively educating individuals with limited access to consistent, quality education. Though not explicitly stated, this perspective appears to support the justification for the hierarchical and autocratic nature of HBCU governance that Minor (2005) describes as strong presidential leadership. Although the lack of HBCU faculty participation in governance may relate to the notoriously heavy teaching loads that may have distracted faculty members from serious engagement, Minor's survey (2005) suggests that HBCU faculty do have some control over curricular decision making.

Beverley Guy-Sheftall (2006), former faculty senate chair at Spelman, observed that Johnnetta B. Cole (then president of Spelman) "actually encouraged faculty to pursue the establishment of formal governance structures" (p. 30). Given her own history as an active, outspoken faculty member, Cole has noted that she believed Spelman would be a stronger institution if more faculty members were involved in institutional decision making (personal communication, August 1, 2009). Guy-Sheftall (2006) also noted that at Spelman the faculty share responsibility in a very real sense for "tenure and promotion policies, faculty hiring, the faculty handbook, curriculum review, faculty grievances, and, most recently, program development and review" (p. 31). She added, "It hasn't always been easy, and it's still a work in progress, but faculty members, with support from the administration [under both Cole and the current president, Beverley Tatum], are exploring more effective, long-term strategies for institutionalizing a new model of shared governance that we hope will be replicated on other campuses of our size, especially at HBCUs" (Guy-Sheftall, 2006, p. 34).

Like Cole, Walter Kimbrough, president of Philander Smith College, worked with the American Association of University Professors to enhance his institution's tenure process, ensure due process in grievances, promote and maintain shared governance, and get his college off the AAUP censure list. Kimbrough believed that one of the quickest ways to ease tension on campus was "to rescind an edict by the former president that prevented faculty and staff from speaking with the media. This directive caused a tenured faculty member to be summarily dismissed and led to the AAUP sanction" (personal communication, August 15, 2009). Because faculty members were entrenched in the previous ways of the institution, Kimbrough said, he had to "push for more faculty involvement, not simply to challenge the 'administration,' but to first start as a self-governing group." He noted that "a strong faculty and a solid academic program are the keys to a strong institution" (personal communication, August 15, 2009).

Perhaps most enlightening and encouraging for the future leadership of HBCUs was Kimbrough's description of his job: "to create a climate where we can engage in spirited discussion and debate in order to develop the best ideas to further the college. My challenge has been to create this climate where we can disagree with each other and there not be any repercussions from disagreeing with the president, which was the case before" (personal communication,

August 15, 2009). Kimbrough also noted that although the current economic crisis has forced Philander Smith College to tighten its belt, the institution has been fortunate in that it has not had to make any cuts in the past few years. Since he arrived at the struggling institution, he has increased faculty salaries consistently; in 2008, faculty received a 7 percent raise. Cole and Kimbrough exemplify leadership that respects faculty contributions and governance, the kind of leadership that is needed at HBCUs (personal communication, August 15, 2009).

Another contextual issue that may hinder shared governance at HBCUs is their financial stability, or rather lack thereof. Grossly underfunded in both the public and private sectors (see Jackson, Snowden, and Eckes, 2002; Minor, 2008), this reality is also offered as justification for strong leadership at HBCUs that has not always incorporated faculty (Minor, 2005).

Interestingly, the research and anecdotes related to faculty governance at HBCUs, though a small body, focus largely on faculty, virtually ignoring administrative perspectives. This lack of exposure may serve to simplify the dialogue on HBCU faculty governance compared with HWIs, especially with regard to the historical but also contemporary institutional contexts.

Although the dialogue on faculty governance at HBCUs is riddled with critique and qualification, Minor (2005) further complicates the issue by suggesting that "given the challenges facing many HBCUs, the focus, arguably, should not simply be on faculty participation, but rather on how such participation can help advance the institution" (p. 35). In essence, this statement elicits consideration of the advantages and drawbacks to faculty governance at HBCUs, with particular attention to intended outcomes for students, faculty, and individual institutions.

General Overview of Faculty Issues

Faculty issues at HBCUs are often characterized in terms of challenges to professional development and promotion (Thompson and Dey, 1998). For instance, multiple scholars have pointed out issues related to socialization, satisfaction, low salaries, high teaching loads, productivity (such as articles in peer-reviewed publications), gender gaps in pay and rank, and lack of shared governance (Agesa, Granger, and Price, 2002; Betsey, 2007; Price, 2007; Renzulli, Grant, and Kathuria, 2006).

Both anecdotal and empirical evidence support significant disparities in faculty experiences at HBCUs and HWIs, more generally as well as with emphases on academic subject areas (Agesa, Granger, and Price, 2002; Betsey, 2007; Price, 2007; Renzulli, Grant, and Kathuria, 2006). Regardless, most of the literature points to the lack of faculty socialization at HBCUs (Johnson, 2001; Johnson and Harvey, 2002). Although HBCU faculty acknowledge and appreciate clear institutional expectations and policies related to promotion and tenure, they simultaneously note the lack of socialization by senior faculty (Johnson and Harvey, 2002). In fact, the literature consistently suggests that heavy teaching loads serve as a deterrent to more explicit faculty mentoring for individuals on the tenure track.

Although these challenges to faculty life at HBCUs are a reality, HBCUs are able to celebrate major success in terms of producing a large number of African American faculty members (see Perna, 2001). In addition, HBCUs have played and continue to play a critical role in producing African American female faculty in the STEM fields (Perna and others, 2009; Solorzano, 1995).

For various reasons stemming from financial instability, HBCUs have long underpaid their faculty members (U.S. Department of Education, 2009b; Provasnik, Shafer, and Snyder, 2004). According to the U.S. Department of Education, since the 1976–77 academic year, full-time instructional faculty members at HBCUs have received salaries that are approximately 80 percent of those at all institutions (Provasnik, Shafer, and Snyder, 2004). Furthermore, although HBCUs are more gender equitable in terms of men's and women's pay across the board, the disparities in average salary at HBCUs and HWIs are significant, even when accounting for sector, size, and selectivity (Renzulli, Grant, and Kathuria, 2006). In fact, the constraints on faculty salaries in the most underresourced HBCUs appear to serve as a dampening effect on the gender wage gap. Consequently, the largest wage gaps at HBCUs are observed at the most elite (and generally better resourced) HBCUs, mirroring the disparities found in HWIs (Renzulli, Grant, and Kathuria, 2006).

Although the literature on faculty at HBCUs is often based on aggregate data, a small but growing body of work focuses on specific academic subject areas. For example, Stier's study of physical education faculty at HBCUs (1992) identifies important connections between receipt of the doctoral degree, teaching and research responsibilities, full- and part-time status, prior teaching and coaching experience, and gender issues. In fact, this research sheds light on such important issues as the perpetuation of traditional gender norms in faculty hiring found in more gender-related research (see Bonner, 2001; Gasman, 2007b).

Along similar lines, some research exists on the satisfaction and productivity among African American female faculty in nursing at HBCUs (McNeal, 2003). Although HBCUs have a history of marginalizing African American women (Gasman, 2007b), this research sheds light on successes. In fact, McNeal (2003) found that a higher percentage of HBCU faculty reported holding deanships or program coordinator positions, received a higher number of grant awards, and held more professional leadership positions when compared with their same-race, same-gender peers at HWIs. This research also supports the findings from more general literature on HBCU faculty, noting dissatisfaction with faculty mentoring and socialization (Johnson and Harvey, 2002) and suggesting that at least in some cases, faculty issues at HBCUs and HWIs may be similar.

A more robust area of research on academic fields at HBCUs focuses on economics—that is, HBCUs' role in producing economics faculty members and in producing HBCU economics faculty members compared with their HWI peers. Framed with the assumption that research productivity is an important social good for academicians, especially those providing an African American perspective, numerous scholars focus on the role of HBCU economics faculty as both teachers and academics. According to Agesa, Granger, and Price (2002), the heavy focus on teaching is a "major impediment to research output of economists at HBCUs" (p. 88). Interestingly, this research supports the notion that increased grant money from organizations such as the National Science Foundation for HBCU economists explicitly enables these faculty members to improve their productivity in terms of published articles in refereed economics publications (Price, 2007). In the case of economics, faculty exposure through publications is thought to shed light on the African American perspective, though this idea has barely been examined empirically (Betsey, 2007).

Research on specific academic fields at HBCUs provides an important perspective and adds substance to the nuanced HBCU context. Although these studies often provide a snapshot in time of one discipline, these contributions support past research, especially with regard to hiring and wage disparities between the genders, for example. Additional research on other academic disciplines and following up on economics, nursing, and physical education may prove important in terms of understanding related tangential issues surrounding HBCU faculty such as diversity, governance, and socialization.

HBCUs are often referred to as focusing on four-year institutions, and virtually no research exists on two-year HBCU faculty and the challenges they face. Based on the existing literature on two-year colleges and on HBCUs, certain issues at these institutions related to full- or part-time teaching status, research expectations, academic subject area, gender, institution size, student demographic and academic backgrounds, and governance are ripe for research.

Fundraising

D O RAISING PRIVATE FUNDS for an HBCU and raising those same funds for an HWI differ markedly? If provided adequate resources, would HBCUs be able to garner the same or similar alumni giving rates? Research tends to support the notion that commonalities exist in asking for donations for any and all philanthropic causes, regardless of an organization's ethnic makeup and orientation (Walton and Gasman, 2008). Advancement professionals at HBCUs, however, constantly face a distinctive set of challenges that are often taken for granted at other mainstream institutions of higher learning.

Consider this: at a major gift fundraising training session a few years ago, a group of African American development officers from various HBCUs sat attentively for two days listening as an HWI instructor discussed the steps to identifying, cultivating, soliciting, and stewarding an individual for a major gift. She explained that unlike an annual gift, where the thought process is relatively quick and usually results in a donation from the donor's disposable income, the major gift is typically ten times the size, has been given careful consideration, and is appropriate to one's capacity. Often, the final donation will incorporate the input of family members and, in some cases, a financial advisor. Each example the instructor gave referenced a case study featuring a former student, now working for a Fortune 500 company, from whom her advancement office had successfully secured a multimillion-dollar gift.

Upon hearing this impressive story, one audience participant asked, "If one college or department is nurturing a donor of such caliber and another area of the university is pursuing that same person, who should be allowed to continue the cultivation?" The facilitator without any hesitation said, "Not to worry, just move on to the next donor; there are plenty of them out there." Although this type of cordial donor sharing may be an accepted policy at many majority institutions where the quantity of wealthy donors may be vast, the reality at most HBCUs is very different. Rather than an enormous pool of prosperous candidates, HBCUs have a much smaller assortment of alumni and therefore affluent individuals, forcing these institutions to flip a coin to decide who gets to pursue the donor. This situation often leaves the losing side relying on contributors to the annual fund. Why does this situation happen? Perhaps it can be attributed to the fact that HWIs are larger and graduate a higher number of individuals from affluent families and are predisposed to the idea of philanthropy (Gasman and Anderson-Thompkins, 2003).

A History of Fundraising

Because fundraising often manifests itself differently in the HBCU community, some scholars have paid particular attention to both the history and contemporary fundraising situation at these institutions. Gasman (2008a) examined the history of perhaps the most important organization involved in fundraising at HBCUs, the United Negro College Fund. Specifically, she explored the institution's strategies for raising money from various constituencies, its use of images, and the role of HBCU presidents in moving the organization's perspective on race relations and leadership forward.

Continuing an interest in the strategies for fundraising in the black college community and the racial dynamics of raising funds in the mid-twentieth century, Gasman and Drezner (2008, 2009a, 2009b) explored the work of the Oram Group, a for-profit fundraising organization with a penchant for working with HBCUs. Gasman and Drezner focused their attention on several historic campaigns at HBCUs and the role of leadership, boards of trustees, and community relations in fundraising.

Interestingly, this historical research reveals discrimination by corporations and foundations allocating funds to higher education, with HBCUs, save for a few examples, garnering substantially less money in their efforts to raise funds (Gasman and Drezner, 2008). Moreover, Gasman and Drezner (2008, 2009a, 2009b) found that HBCUs have not solicited their alumni in any systematic way, believing that this population did not have access to funds. Of note, the research related to the history of fundraising at HBCUs boasts similar findings to that about the contemporary fundraising situation at these institutions: low percentages of alumni participation in giving, small endowments, and a lack of fundraising infrastructure.

Alumni Giving

Scholars studying current fundraising patterns and activities in the HBCU context, like their historian counterparts, have found that HBCUs do not engage their alumni aggressively in the giving process (Gasman and Anderson-Thompkins, 2003). This finding is supported by the dismal alumni giving percentages for HBCUs reported annually in the college edition of *U.S. News & World Report*. For years, these institutions have enrolled students, nurtured and guided their academic matriculation, and requested nothing more upon graduation than a final payment to ensure a zero balance on their accounts (Gasman and Anderson-Thompkins, 2003). The process behind this line of thinking is typically that HBCU students are poor and saddled with massive loans so they need time (about ten years) to get on their feet, start their families, and establish their careers (Gasman and Anderson-Thompkins, 2003).

Black colleges like the black church, which for centuries provided social, cultural, spiritual, educational, and philanthropic development for African Americans, could parlay this similar connection into a lifelong union. Traditionally in the black church, the majority of African Americans are taught from a young age that they have an obligation to give to the church; black colleges would do well to engage in this kind of teaching as well (Holloman, Gasman, and Anderson-Thompkins, 2003). With a large percentage of HBCU undergraduates first-generation college students compared with the national average, these institutions could easily take on the role of a churchlike organization, as many students are experiencing the outside world for the first time and longing for the guidance and organizational closeness usually provided by their church back home (Holloman, Gasman, and Anderson-Thompkins, 2003). It is not a coincidence that the black church has been the center of African American giving and the single most effective fundraising mechanism for blacks (Byrd, 1990; Fairfax, 1995; Frazier, 1963, 1977; Lincoln, 1974; Pressley, 1995). According to Hall-Russell (1999), "African Americans are experts at educating their prospective donors in the church setting" (p. 7). When a revered figure in the community such as a pastor appeals on behalf of a charitable cause, blacks are more likely to contribute financially. According to researchers, the leaders of HBCUs need to emulate this kind of success, teaching their potential donors early in their educational process (Holloman, Gasman, and Anderson-Thompkins, 2003). Like trusted pastors, HBCU leaders such as presidents and advancement staff need to have prestige and credibility in the community—especially the immediate African American community. One of the strongest motivators for black college giving is the leadership and charisma of the institutional president (Hall-Russell and Kasberg, 1997). Perhaps it is linked in some way to the same leadership and dynamism that is displayed in the African American church. Like the black church pastor, the HBCU president has to be compelling in his or her presentation. The president must inspire his or her people to act. And it is accomplished by presenting crucial issues to the audience using compelling language (Gasman and Anderson-Thompkins, 2003).

Educating Alumni Early

HBCU graduates are frequently asked what the turning point was in their lives and when things began to make sense for them. Many say it was during their college years. Had the idea of giving back been introduced to students during freshman orientation along with service-learning projects and student alumni association activities, the alumni's sense of commitment and obligation would have formed a foundation, thereby cementing a strong bond and perhaps a financial affinity for their undergraduate institution. Along this line, Drezner (2008) examined the activities of the United Negro College Fund's National Pre-Alumni Council, which encourages current students at private HBCUs to raise funds for their colleges. NPAC has been successful in encouraging students to give back and educating them about philanthropic giving and its role in sustaining HBCUs.

Issues of Infrastructure

Another basis for the immense disparity between fundraising at HWIs and HBCUs, according to research, stems from the lack of resources required to assemble a high-performing development operation (Gasman and Anderson-Thompkins, 2003). Under ideal conditions, these resources would include key personnel, ongoing education and professional training, and technical assistance. Whereas many HWIs have these components in abundance stemming from large endowments that for decades have produced discretionary income that is used for training and infrastructure, most HBCUs do not. The luxury of having tools to identify affluent alumni that may lie beneath the surface wanting the institution to initiate a courtship typically does not exist at HBCUs (Gasman and Anderson-Thompkins, 2003). Staffs are usually very small, and in many cases those assigned to undertake these new "other duties as assigned" are inexperienced when it comes to formal fundraising (Gasman and Anderson-Thompkins, 2003).

When certain black colleges have been afforded the tools to create more diverse portfolios for financial resources and stronger infrastructure, they have dramatically increased their advancement operation capacity and alumni giving rates. Consider, for example, that in 2001, the Kresge Foundation awarded $18 million to five black colleges (Bethune-Cookman College, Dillard University, Johnson C. Smith University, Meharry Medical College, and Xavier University). As a result, the schools collectively hired sixty development staff, financed new and ongoing technical and professional support, and purchased computers and database management software (Gasman and Anderson-Thompkins, 2003). Today each of these institutions is much stronger in fundraising, having the proper infrastructure to pursue donors and manage donations.

Endowment Size

Another area of concern scholars highlight is the size of HBCU endowments. Of the nation's 105 HBCUs, only three have endowments in the top three hundred: Howard University, Spelman College, and Hampton University. Low endowments mean fewer dollars available for operating costs and institutional financial aid. HBCU endowments are lower than those of their HWI counterparts for a variety of reasons. HWIs suffer from a history of unequal state and federal funding. In addition, as mentioned, over the course of their history foundation and corporate support has been less for black than for white institutions; historically white institutions have received substantially more money even when size is taken into account. Another disadvantage, also mentioned above, stems from the fact that alumni giving to HBCUs, which is critical to building endowments, has been and continues to be lower on average than to HWIs. As mentioned, these lower rates are partly because of African Americans' historic lack of access to wealth as a result of systemic forms of racism throughout American history (Gasman and Sedgwick, 2005). That said, scholars have urged HBCUs to take more responsibility in the area of fundraising.

Advancement staff at public state-funded black colleges often have an even harder time raising funds than their privately funded counterparts as a result of misconceptions about public higher education institutions. According to Dwayne Ashley, president of the Thurgood Marshall College Fund (a consortium of public black colleges), "People hear the word 'public' and think the state is funding [the institutions] 100 percent. . . . They think, 'I pay taxes, and that should cover the resources.' But state funding is never more than 30 to 40 percent, leaving public HBCUs to raise the rest" (Ashley, 2001, p. 19). Second, state-funded black colleges suffer twice. Many donors who give to the United Negro College Fund assume that they are supporting all black colleges, when they are actually supporting only the thirty-nine member institutions—none of which are public. The Thurgood Marshall College Fund, founded in 1987 by N. Joyce Payne, represents the country's forty-five public black colleges.

Overall, the research on fundraising for HBCUs is sparse, and many questions are still unanswered. The area is ripe for exploration; these institutions would benefit immensely from additional scholarship pertaining to campaigns, presidential leadership and fundraising, success models, and building endowments.

Federal and State Policy

THE FEDERAL GOVERNMENT maintains a powerful position of influence at all levels of education, despite the fact that this area of social welfare is generally considered the jurisdiction of the states. Throughout the education landscape, federal policy priorities are brought to bear principally through the ebb and flow of financial support (Richardson and Harris, 2004). With respect to federal and state policy toward HBCUs, a range of executive orders and legislation have been instrumental in their development and, quite arguably, their underdevelopment.

Legislation

Federal legislation has had a substantial impact on the development of historically black colleges and universities, prompting expansion and curriculum development. This legislative support manifests in myriad ways over the course of history.

Freedmen's Bureau Acts

Congress passed the first major legislation to shape the education of blacks with the Freedmen's Bureau Acts of 1865 and 1868, which established the Bureau of Refugees, Freedmen, and Abandoned Lands as an agency in the War Department. Providing education assistance was among a range of responsibilities with which the Freedmen's Bureau was charged in support of former slaves. Over the course of its seven-year existence and with limited political and public support, the Freedmen's Bureau helped found several black colleges, including

Howard University (1867), Hampton University (1868), and Clark Atlanta University (1867) (Lieberman, 1994; Parker, 1954).

Land-Grant Colleges Act

In an effort to expand higher education, in 1862, Congress passed the National Land-Grant Colleges Act, commonly known as the Morrill Act, which gave states federal land to use or sell in order to establish and fund institutions that would "teach such branches of learning as are related to agricultural and mechanical arts" (7 U.S.C. 301 *et seq.*). Given that this legislation preceded emancipation, it is remarkable that three black institutions—Alcorn State University (Mississippi), Hampton University (Virginia), and Claflin University (South Carolina)—received funds from the Morrill Act of 1862. More common was a blatant disregard for black higher education by southern states, which directed nearly all funds to white institutions that barred African Americans (Thelin, 2004). With the passage of the second Morrill Act in 1890, southern states were compelled to support black higher education, as the new legislation stated that "No money shall be paid out under this act to any State or Territory for the support and maintenance of a college where a distinction of race or color is made in the admission of students, but the establishment and maintenance of such colleges separately for white and colored students shall be held to be in compliance with the provisions of this act if the funds received in such State or Territory be equitably divided" (7 U.S.C. 322 *et seq.*). With that, federal policy assured land-grant education for blacks and, at the same time, affirmed the "separate but equal" doctrine of the era. As a result, black land-grant institutions were established in each southern state (see Exhibit 1).

Subsequent legislation related to land-grant institutions such as the Adams Act (1906), Smith-Lever Act (1914), and the Smith-Hughes Act (1917) had limited financial impact on the 1890 land-grant institutions, which were grossly underfunded relative to their white counterparts for the first seventy-seven years of their existence (Humphries, 1991). In 1967, however, this policy of neglect was reversed, with passage of Public Law 89–106, followed by the Food and Agriculture Act of 1977, and Public Law 97–98 in 1981, all of which granted federal funding to the historically black land-grant institutions

EXHIBIT 1
1890 Land-Grant Colleges and Universities

Alabama A&M University
Alcorn State University (Mississippi)
Delaware State University
Florida A&M University
Fort Valley State University (Georgia)
Kentucky State University[a]
Langston University (Oklahoma)
Lincoln University (Missouri)[a]
North Carolina A&T University
Prairie View A&M University (Texas)
South Carolina State University
Southern University and A&M, Baton Rouge (Louisiana)
Tennessee State University
Tuskegee University (Alabama)[b]
University of Arkansas at Pine Bluff
University of Maryland, Eastern Shore
Virginia State University
West Virginia State College[a]

[a] Currently more than 50 percent white.
[b] Private but created by state legislature; often considered a land-grant institution.
Sources: Cooperative State Research, Education, and Extension Service (n.d.); Christy and Williamson, 1992, p. 57.

(Humphries, 1991; Christy and Williamson, 1992) and served to bolster their development.

GI Bill

From 1936 to 1947, the total enrollment at HBCUs increased 118 percent, from thirty-four thousand to seventy-four thousand students. Moreover, in fall 1947, an estimated 35 percent of HBCU students were black World War II veterans who were taking advantage of what has been touted as the "greatest piece of social legislation" of its era (Onkst, 1998, p. 517). The GI Bill of Rights, enacted in 1944 as the Serviceman's Readjustment Act, offered federal financial aid to individuals (that is, eligible World War II veterans) for the first time and enabled thousands of blacks to undertake postsecondary education (Onkst, 1998).

The unconventional federal program relied on a conventional administration strategy that gave states the authority to manage many of the GI educational benefits, thus keeping intact the explicit discrimination that limited African Americans' access to educational options, particularly in the South. In fact, despite the impressive enrollment figures cited earlier, by 1947 the states' longstanding practice of underfunding HBCUs resulted in an estimated twenty thousand black veterans' being turned away by black colleges because of a shortage of facilities and resources (Turner and Bound, 2003). In total, black veterans accounted for only 4 percent of servicemen using the GI Bill's education benefits in 1946–47, even though a 1944 poll had shown that 43 percent of blacks were interested in furthering their education after the war versus 29 percent of whites (Onkst, 1998; Turner and Bound, 2003). It can certainly be argued that the GI Bill created a climate that fostered African American educational aspirations, helped raise the overall postsecondary attainment of African Americans, and possibly led to racial demographic shifts at some of the nation's colleges and universities. The impact of the legislation on HBCUs should not be overstated, however, considering the potential of these institutions had equitable structures existed to absorb the returning servicemen.

Civil Rights Act of 1964

By 1961, only 17 percent of white public colleges in the South had admitted black students, with the overwhelming majority of black college students still attending HBCUs (U.S. Department of Education, 1984). Up to that point, the legislative tenor regarding education allowed for segregation and inequitable distribution of federal funds while still attempting to promote broad access. Title VI of the Civil Rights Act of 1964, however, helped to broaden the range of educational options available to African Americans by requiring that "no person in the United States shall, on the ground of race, color, or national origin, be excluded from participation in, or be denied the benefits of, or be subjected to discrimination under any program or activity receiving Federal financial assistance" (P.L. 88–52, 78 Stat. 241). Through this measure, Congress pressured institutions to desegregate or incur financial sanctions, in effect giving the federal government jurisdiction over the dismantling of state systems of segregation. Accordingly, the Office of Civil Rights in the Department of Health, Education and Welfare—now the Department of Education—was created to monitor compliance with Title VI. As states were now required to develop and implement desegregation plans, compliance with Title VI became the impetus for the epic state-level desegregation litigation mentioned previously.

Higher Education Act of 1965

Although Title VI targeted higher education indirectly, the Higher Education Act of 1965 (HEA) and its subsequent reauthorizations define the federal government's policy toward postsecondary education. As part of President Lyndon Johnson's Great Society programs, the legislation sought to improve the quality of and access to higher education by granting aid to eligible institutions as well as individuals in the "first comprehensive federal assistance policy designed for higher education" (Green, 2004, p. 71).

Title III of the Higher Education Act of 1965

Title III of the HEA, originally called "Strengthening Developing Institutions," acknowledged the value of HBCUs and other institutions "struggling for survival" and "isolated from the main currents of academic life" (P.L. 89–329, 79 Stat. 1229) by providing them with direct federal aid. The 1986 amendment of the HEA signaled a more explicit commitment to HBCUs through the creation of the first formula grant program under Title III, Part B, Strengthening Historically Black Colleges and Universities (Boren and others, 1987). The U.S. Department of Education's *Biennial Evaluation Report for Fiscal Years 1995–1996* states that Part B is "designed to help improve the programs and management of HBCUs and to enhance educational opportunities for students. It is also intended to facilitate a decrease in reliance on government financial support and to encourage reliance on endowments and private sources" (U.S. Department of Education, 1996, p. 26). Part B funds are currently distributed on a formula basis through both the Strengthening Historically Black Colleges and Universities Program and the Strengthening Historically Black Graduate Institutions Program. The awards can be used for such projects as facilities improvement, faculty professional development, student services, and the purchase of scientific equipment. Amendments to the HEA in 1992 and 1998 created the HBCU Capital Financing Program and added the Minority Science and Engineering Improvement Program under Part D and Part E, respectively, of Title III, both of which provide additional direct aid to HBCUs (P.L. 105–244).

In 2007, the College Cost Reduction and Access Act (P.L. 110–84) was enacted, amending Title III to include Part F, Mandatory Appropriations for Minority-Serving Institutions. The act provided $85 million of supplemental funding to HBCUs for fiscal years 2008 and 2009; however, authorization for this aid expired at the end of fiscal year 2009.

The most recent comprehensive reauthorization of HEA, the Higher Education Opportunity Act of 2008 (P.L. 110–315), created a new institutional grant program under Part A of Title III to support "predominantly black institutions" as defined therein. The act also amended Part A of Title VII to include institutional grant programs to support master's degree programs at specific HBCUs and predominantly black institutions.

Since its inception in 1965 and particularly as a result of the 1986 amendment creating the Part B, Strengthening HBCUs Program, the Higher Education Act has provided substantial support to HBCUs (Figure 1). Minor (2008) suggests, however, that this type of funding is more or less institutional "financial aid . . rather than purposeful investment" (p. 32). As an example, he notes that the average Title III award to HBCUs in 2006 amounted to $2 million per institution, a figure that does little to close the persistent funding gaps between HBCUs and HWIs.

Likewise, Wolanin (1998) raised an important policy question about the intended duration of direct support for HBCUs. Referring to a 1985 prepared statement, he noted that "advocates for the creation of Part B in 1985–86 also argued that Part B would be a ten-year program" (p. 24). A 2008 Congressional Research Service report also conceded that because one purpose of Title III programs is "to improve the fiscal stability and self-sufficiency of the participating institutions," questions as to the success or continued existence of these programs could be raised (Mercer, 2008, p. 15).

Based on its budgetary history, there generally seems to be strong political support for Title III, and the literature does not currently reflect a preoccupation

FIGURE 1
Federal Direct Aid to Institutions (HEA Title III Appropriations)

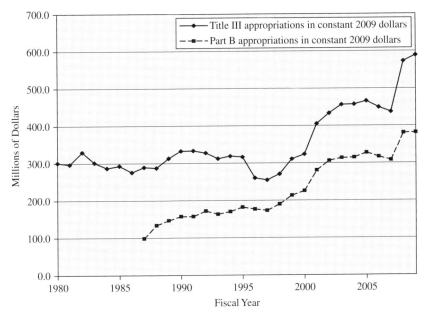

Source: U.S. Department of Education, 2008.

with questions about its justifiability. Nevertheless, HBCUs must highlight the successes of the Part B program with respect to its other stated goals—improved curricular offerings, management, and facilities as well as enhanced educational opportunities for students.

Executive Orders and the White House Initiative on HBCUs

Even before the 1986 amendment to the HEA that created the Strengthening Historically Black Colleges and Universities Program, President Jimmy Carter introduced the federal policy shift toward unambiguous support of HBCUs in 1980 with Executive Order 12232. The order established a federal initiative "to overcome the effects of discriminatory treatment and to strengthen and expand the capacity of historically Black colleges and universities to provide quality education." Each president since Carter has replaced his predecessor's HBCU executive order with his own—renewing, adapting, or expanding the program to increase participation by HBCUs in federally sponsored programs.

Executive Order 12320, signed by President Reagan in 1981, expanded Carter's original program by formalizing the logistics by which government agencies would execute the program. It required an annual federal plan for assistance to historically black colleges and an annual federal performance report on executive agency actions to assist historically black colleges, both comprising input from participating government agencies. Reagan's order also called for an effort to "stimulate initiatives by private sector businesses and institutions to strengthen historically black colleges and universities."

With the signing of Executive Order 12677 in 1989, President George H.W. Bush took the program a step further by creating the President's Board of Advisors on HBCUs. Bush also defined the White House Initiative on HBCUs as an organization in the Department of Education to assist the advisory commission, act as "liaison between the Executive branch and historically black colleges and universities" and help facilitate the program. Bush's executive order was also less retrospective, doing away with previous language that defined as an objective of the program "[overcoming] the effects of discriminatory treatment." Finally, Bush also emphasized using the program to help increase the number of HBCU faculty and graduates in science and technology.

President Clinton's 1993 HBCU executive order, 12876, restated President Bush's order with few revisions. Most significant, President Clinton added a new layer of accountability to ensure agencies' compliance with the program. Although agencies had been required since Reagan to report their annual performance, with Clinton, the report now had to "measure performance against the objectives set forth in its annual plan" and was to be submitted to the Office of Management and Budget, which would be "responsible for overseeing compliance with the Annual Federal Plan."

President George W. Bush signed the latest edition of this executive order, 13256, in 2002. He removed the previous two administrations' programmatic focus on science and technology and revoked President Clinton's compliance measure requiring agencies to submit annual performance reports to the Office of Management and Budget. Under President Bush's order, the President's

Board of Advisors on HBCUs was required to submit an annual report to the President "on results of the participation of HBCUs in federal programs" and new emphasis was placed on developing such opportunities as student and faculty doctoral fellowships, international exchange, and study-abroad programs.

Despite the well-intentioned verbiage and stated goals of these executive orders, the evidence suggests that the White House Initiative has had little effect over time on the level of federal grant awards to HBCUs relative to HWIs (Minor, 2008). In fact, Minor (2008) found that although federal funding for all institutions of higher education increased 40 percent during the period from 1993 to 2002, funding to HBCUs increased only 24 percent. Not surprisingly, some higher education professionals have recommended reorganization and reconstitution of the White House Initiative (Minor, 2008).

Howard University

Any thoughtful discussion of federal policy toward HBCUs must take into account the unique status of Howard University, located in Washington, D.C. Founded as Howard Normal and Theological Institute for the Education of Teachers and Preachers in 1867, federally chartered and named for the commissioner of the Freedmen's Bureau, Howard has maintained a special relationship with the federal government since its inception. Until 1873, Howard was supported primarily by budget appropriations from the Freedmen's Bureau. In 1879, Congress began annual appropriations to Howard, the first of which amounted to $10,000 (B. Cole, 1977; Wolanin, 1998). Initial budget appropriations were subject to an annual congressional vote until 1928, when Congress amended the Incorporation Act of Howard University to authorize annual appropriations to "aid in the construction, development, improvement and maintenance of the University" (20 U.S.C. 123; B. Cole, 1977; Logan, 1969). The most recent federal appropriations to Howard University and its hospital are detailed in Exhibit 2.

State Policies Toward HBCUs

Although federal policy has played a major role in shaping the prospects of HBCUs, states have an arguably more direct policy position, especially for

EXHIBIT 2
Howard University Appropriations History

Fiscal Year	Appropriation (Thousands Of Dollars)
2001	232,474
2002	237,474
2003	238,440
2004	238,763
2005	238,789
2006	237,392
2007	233,865
2008	233,245
2009	234,977

Source: U.S. Department of Education, 2009c.

publicly funded institutions. One well-documented aspect of states' policies toward public black colleges has been the historic funding disparities that have contributed significantly to their much slower development. For example, several scholars have called attention to the persistent funding discrimination experienced by the black land-grant colleges relative to their white counterparts (Humphries, 1991; Craig, 1991, 1992; Kujovich, 1993; Jenkins, 1942; Christy and Williamson, 1992). Kujovich (1993) reported that up until the 1940s, "state legislatures favored their White land grants in both state appropriations and the distribution of federal funds" (p. 78); for land-grant functions such as military training, extension services, and research, funding was "virtually nonexistent" (p. 78). As late as 1968, black land-grant colleges received only 9.7 percent of funding to land-grant institutions (Humphries, 1991).

Similarly, a recent report on public HBCUs presents state funding data for four-year public institutions across four southern states (Minor, 2008). The findings support the claim that state-level funding disparities persist between HBCUs and HWIs, in total appropriations as well as per student. For instance, Minor (2008) found that although North Carolina provided North Carolina State University and the University of North Carolina–Chapel Hill close to

$15,700 per student, North Carolina A&T and Fayetteville State University (both HBCUs) received only $7,800 per student. Also worth noting, however, is North Carolina's engagement on this issue, as the state has developed a funding initiative to address the growth capacity of its public HBCUs (Minor, 2008).

Nevertheless, such funding inequities provided momentum for NAACP-led desegregation litigation as well as cases related to Title VI compliance. States have been required to develop policies that comply with federal law and related court rulings, though no single specific strategy has been prescribed. Thus, the states' desegregation settlements and plans include a variety of policy approaches: providing funding to HBCUs for new facilities and academic programs, standardizing mission statements and admissions criteria across the state's system of higher education, and minimizing program duplication and racial identifiability across the state's system. In some cases, these policies have led to closure or merger of HBCUs (M. C. Brown, 2001; Brown, Donahoo, and Bertrand, 2001; Brown and Freeman, 2004; Williams, 1988).

Perhaps one of the most pressing concerns for HBCUs regarding state funding is the potentially detrimental impact of trending declines in appropriations across all higher education institutions that began during the recession of the late 1980s and continue today (Mumper and Freeman, 2005). As black colleges generally garner smaller revenues from tuition, grants, contracts, and gifts than do predominantly white colleges, state budget shortfalls that result in cuts in higher education funding affect HBCUs more profoundly (Jackson and Nunn, 2003). Therefore, these institutions must maintain a considerable focus on financial flexibility so that potential losses in state funding might be absorbed.

The historical framework of federal and state policy toward HBCUs is critical to understanding contemporary HBCU issues. Clearly, the impact of governmental neglect of these institutions has been vast and deep. Less apparent, however, is the impact of policies—from federal direct institutional aid programs to state desegregation policies—on current HBCU student outcomes. Researchers must work to piece together the modern picture of HBCUs, in all its shades and hues, so that policies can be refined, revamped, or discarded to increase postsecondary attainment among an increasingly diverse population.

Curriculum

ARLY CURRICULUM AT HBCUs was a clear response to the immediate needs of former slaves who fervently and resolutely sought education as a means to true liberation (Anderson, 1988). Before emancipation in 1860, the illiteracy rate among blacks was 95 percent. Therefore, basic literacy was the first core curricular objective, not just at primary and secondary schools but also among aspiring black colleges. As illiteracy declined to 70 percent by 1880 and 30 percent in 1910, the curricula at HBCUs evolved to reflect the growing competency of students (Anderson, 1988; Jackson and Nunn, 2003).

By 1915 several black institutions offered curricula beyond the three Rs of the primary grades, and the range of labels adopted by the burgeoning HBCUs—university, college, academy, institute, normal school, seminary, high school, training school, industrial school—suggests a similar variation in the early curricular offerings of these institutions (Fairclough, 2007). According to a report on black institutions (Department of the Interior, 1917), only thirty-one private and two state-funded institutions were found to offer some "college work" in 1915, including Howard University, Fisk University, and Meharry Medical College, which were characterized as being the only "college-grade" institutions for blacks (pp. 16–17). Grossly limited public secondary education constrained the ability of HBCUs to offer higher education broadly, such that even among the few college-level institutions, 79 percent of students were in the secondary and elementary grades (Department of the Interior, 1917). As state-funded secondary education expanded, so did HBCUs' focus on higher education; by 1927 the number of black institutions offering college-level work had increased 133 percent to seventy-seven institutions, including many of the public 1890 land-grant colleges (U.S. Department of Education, 1984).

Although both public and private black colleges largely emphasized teacher and ministerial preparation during the late nineteenth and early twentieth centuries, this era in black education was more notably marked by the ideological debate over the curricular approach to be employed toward this end. The crux of the debate was whether black students would be best served by an industrial or a classical curriculum. Scholars have explored the context and substance of this debate in a range of works (Anderson, 1988; Brown and Freeman, 2004; Jackson and Nunn, 2003).

Among private HBCUs, the debate over curriculum was particularly salient, whereas public institutions—primarily the 1890 land-grant colleges— generally lacked the degree of autonomy afforded their private counterparts (Brown and Freeman, 2004). Anderson (1988) methodically reports perspectives on this debate in terms of institutional type, arguing that institutions founded and operated by African American leaders and religious organizations tended to embrace a classical liberal arts curriculum similar to normal schools and colleges led by northern missionary societies. Alternatively, those HBCUs founded or substantially supported by wealthy industrialists espoused an industrial or practical curriculum (Anderson, 1988; Brown and Freeman, 2004).

The debate about curriculum connoted a broader philosophical question regarding the function of black higher education, which has been consistently represented in the literature by the divergent perspectives of Booker T. Washington and W.E.B. Du Bois (Anderson, 1988; Brown and Freeman, 2004; Du Bois, 1903/2005; Jackson and Nunn, 2003). Washington, a former slave, founder of Tuskegee Institute and prominent alumnus of Hampton Institute whose model of industrial education was acclaimed by southern whites and northern philanthropists, advocated for education that "[dignified] and [glorified] common labor and put brains and skill into the common occupations of life" (Harlan, 1974, p. 584). On the other hand, Du Bois, an intellectual born after emancipation and educated at Fisk and Harvard, championed the type of liberal curriculum he had experienced; he noted that although critical to the uplift of blacks, "work alone will not do unless inspired by the right ideals and guided by intelligence" (Du Bois, 1903/2005, p. 112). Of note, both of these men were interested in the same goal of racial uplift for African Americans.

Whether in affirmation of the industrial philosophy or in mere deference to philanthropic interests, by 1890 all black colleges incorporated some "manual training" or industrial courses into their curricula. For example, Tougaloo operated a plantation and Shaw offered courses in carpentry and joinery for male students, cooking and sewing for females (Fairclough, 2007). Most institutions, however, stopped short of adopting the Hampton-Tuskegee model of emphasizing industrial training above the academic subjects (Anderson, 1988). By the late 1920s, even Hampton and Tuskegee brought their curricula in closer alignment with the "ideological mainstream" (Anderson, 1988, p. 34).

Though the level of specialization was generally narrower, curriculum patterns at black colleges often emulated those at white institutions, as it was widely held that curricular differences would be misjudged as intellectual deficiencies (Daniel and Daniel, 1946). This calculation often failed to mollify early critics who thought black colleges were "handicapped by the tenacity with which they have clung to the classical form of curriculum" (W. M. Cole, 2006, p. 358), a curriculum they deemed superfluous and impractical for black students. Ironically, by the 1960s black colleges were widely criticized for their vocational and professional curricular orientations, a legacy that, in the view of contemporary detractors, has diminished the collective stature of HBCUs (Brown and Freeman, 2004; McGrath, 1965; Reid, 1967).

In "The Curriculum of the Negro College," Daniel and Daniel (1946) highlight the dilemma black colleges faced in designing appropriate curricula to meet the needs of their students, given the difficult milieu of racial inequality. In addition to an adequate course of study, black colleges also had to provide students with experiences, examples, and a campus climate that would prepare them "for both the adjustment to a world which restricts [their] movements due to [their] race . . . and the participation in the struggle for and enjoyment of real freedom and equality yet to be attained" (p. 497). Therefore, what remains inarguable is the deftness with which these institutions were able to accommodate multiple external interests and still offer substantive educational opportunities to meet the needs of their students and the black community at large.

Professional Fields

The classical curriculum of private HBCUs was initially geared toward the training of ministers and quickly shifted to encompass, to a greater degree, the training of teachers (Daniel and Daniel, 1946; Harris, Figgures, and Carter, 1975). Teaching and preaching as occupational choices and course offerings at black colleges must be considered in the social context of the era in which they dominated HBCU campuses. Not only were they virtually the only professional options widely available to African Americans but an especially high demand for black teachers was apparent from the 1870s—when they began replacing northern white teachers—until the 1960s. As an example, Fairclough (2007) notes that although public schools in the South needed about seven thousand new black teachers each year in 1900, "fewer than 2,100 blacks completed any kind of education above the elementary level" that year (p. 167).

Well into the twentieth century, black college graduates opted principally into the teaching profession. A 1942 study found that even among the liberal arts black colleges, up to 80 percent of graduates were likely to become teachers (I. C. Brown, 1942). Likewise, the black land-grant colleges, which were established to focus on the agricultural and mechanical arts, were essentially teacher training institutions during their first seventy-seven years as a result of extreme funding constraints (Craig, 1992; Humphries, 1991). By 1959 more than 70 percent of students at black colleges were still choosing teacher education programs despite the increasing overabundance of black teachers (Brazziel, 1960).

At its height, the teacher training tradition among black colleges produced impressive results. During the 1949–50 academic year, black teachers averaged 4.1 years of college, compared with 3.8 years for whites (Walker, 2001). Yet the preponderance of teacher education also signifies the narrow scope of black higher education before the civil rights movement (see Figure 2, which shows the percentage by discipline of baccalaureate degrees awarded by HBCUs during the 1962–63, 1986–87, and 2006–07 academic years). In 1962–63, not only did education degree-earners—who accounted for 52 percent of all HBCU graduates—expect to become teachers but a "considerable proportion" of the natural science, social science, and humanities baccalaureates would have also entered the high school teaching ranks (McGrath, 1965, p. 84).

FIGURE 2
HBCU Baccalaureate Degree Awards by Field

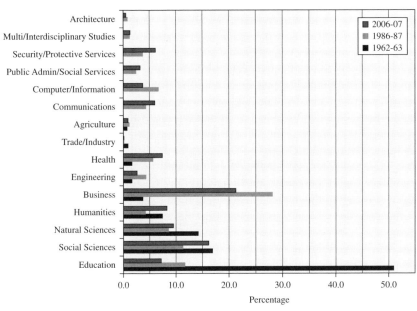

Source: McGrath, 1969, p. 83; U.S. Department of Education, 2009a.

Policy shifts in the mid-1960s finally eased restrictions in occupational opportunities for blacks, increased funding to black colleges and their students, and generally fostered an era of advancement and upward mobility for African Americans. Consequently, the extent of curricular offerings, major selections, and degree awards at black colleges expanded. By 1986–87 the portion of education baccalaureate degrees had decreased to only 11.7 percent, while business-related degree awards increased to 28.1 percent. Twenty years later, in 2006–07, the data still reflect the broader career prospects of African Americans, with significant increases in health professions, communications, and social science fields. The figure also shows that in 2006–07, the STEM fields accounted for 16.3 percent of HBCU baccalaureates, which is particularly significant, given that STEM fields accounted for 15.1 percent of baccalaureate degrees awarded at all U.S. institutions of higher education during the same academic year.

Graduate Work

The evolution of graduate and professional programs at black colleges can be traced to the privately controlled HBCUs. By 1915, among the 2,600 students doing college-level work at black institutions, about 38 percent were enrolled in first professional programs at Howard and Meharry in fields such as medicine, dentistry, pharmacy, and law (U.S. Department of the Interior, 1917). The growth of graduate education at black colleges was initially slow relative to undergraduate programs; however, only five private institutions offered courses of study at the master's degree level before 1937 (Jenkins, 1947). Jenkins (1947) reported on the subsequent increase in master's programs during the 1940s, which resulted in part from shifting certification requirements for secondary teachers as well as the 1938 U.S. Supreme Court decision in *Gaines* v. *Canada.*

By 1946 the number of public black colleges offering graduate-level work exceeded that of private institutions, with education being the foremost curricular area at both types. Figure 3 shows the progression of graduate

FIGURE 3
Number of HBCUs Offering Graduate-Level Programs by Institutional Type

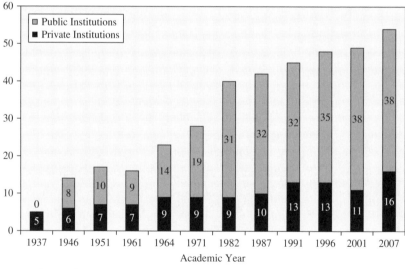

Sources: Jenkins, 1946, p. 236; Jenkins, 1947, p. 300; McGrath, 1965, pp. 172–177; U.S. Department of Education, 2009a.

education at HBCUs since 1937 in terms of the number of public and private institutions that maintain programs. As late as the 2006–07 academic year, fifty-four HBCUs, roughly 52 percent, offered courses of study leading to a master's, doctorate, or first professional degree (for example, law, dentistry, medicine, pharmacy) (U.S. Department of Education, 2009a).

In 2006–07, education degrees accounted for 35 percent of master's and 43 percent of doctoral degree conferred at HBCUs, while STEM fields accounted for 10 percent of master's and 14 percent of doctoral degrees (U.S. Department of Education, 2009a). At the master's level, public administration, social services, and business were also significant, at 17 percent for public administration and 10 percent for social services. Most first professional degrees were awarded in health-related or clinical fields (49 percent) and law (33 percent) (U.S. Department of Education, 2009a).

Black Medical Schools and Medical Education

Even after the Civil War, only a few HWIs in the North would, on occasion, take black medical students. Those in the South refused blacks entry as a rule; blacks had to create their own medical programs (Savitt, 2006; Reitzes and Elkhanialy, 1976). This discrimination led to the establishment of a medical school at Howard University in Washington, D.C., in 1868. Like many black colleges (unless forbidden by state law), Howard accepted both black and white students in its medical school. Howard held the distinction that it was the first medical school to enroll blacks below the Mason-Dixon Line (Watson, 1999). Also of note, unlike white medical schools, Howard accepted women in its medical school (Watson, 1999). Shortly after Howard University started a medical school, Meharry Medical College was created in Nashville, Tennessee, in 1876 (it was originally called the medical department of Central Tennessee College). In addition to these schools, myriad small black medical schools, mainly proprietary in nature, appeared throughout the South (Watson, 1999; Savitt, 2006).

In 1910, Abraham Flexner, working on behalf of the American Medical Association and the Carnegie Foundation for the Advancement of Teaching, issued a report that examined the state of American medical education and led to vast reforms in the way doctors were trained. The Flexner report also led to the closing of most rural medical schools and all but two of the nation's black medical colleges—Meharry and Howard. Even those two schools almost "closed their doors as organized medicine and medical philanthropies pushed the educational reforms promoted by Flexner beyond the capacities of the black institutions to change" (Savitt, 2006, p. 252). Flexner argued that black medical schools made no meaningful contribution to the health problems of blacks, were wasting money, and were producing physicians who lacked substantial training and had received an inadequate education. Based on Flexner's report, Meharry and Howard medical schools would be left to educate enough doctors to serve a population of twelve million blacks in the segregated society of the turn of the century. It would not be until 1975 when Morehouse College established a medical program that the nation would see another black medical school. (The program is known today as the Morehouse School of Medicine and is a separate entity from Morehouse College.)

Another institution of note in medical education is Xavier University of Louisiana. This small black college located in New Orleans is responsible for sending more African Americans to medical school than any other institution in the country. And, of note, the institution accepts many students who would have difficulty pursuing a premedicine curriculum at historically white institutions. These students have lower grade point averages and SAT scores yet are able to successfully secure a place in medical school and pass board exams because of the intensive science education they receive at Xavier. The institution is a model for all colleges and universities in terms of its ability to cultivate future doctors. Overall, HBCUs have a significantly better track record for sending young African Americans to medical school. This success is often attributed to HBCUs' efforts to foster a collaborative rather than competitive climate in the sciences (Perna and others, 2007).

Engineering at HBCUs

Although HBCUs have had considerable success preparing African Americans to assume roles in a range of professional fields—from teaching to medicine, business to military service—one additional curricular area gaining scholarly attention with respect to HBCUs is engineering. The growing need for high-tech talent coupled with the persistent underrepresentation of African Americans in this area make the record of the relatively few HBCU engineering programs more noteworthy. In fact, the demonstrated capacity of HBCUs to deliver engineering education could represent a critical argument in the case for their continued support.

Engineering education in the United States officially began with the founding of the Military Academy at West Point in 1802, but its subsequent growth was gradual up to the enactment of the first Morrill Act of 1862. From 1862 to 1872, the number of engineering schools increased from twelve to seventy and engineering education entered a "period of consistent development," with the systemization of curricula, diversification of disciplines, and emergence of professional societies (Grayson, 1980, p. 379). National accreditation for engineering education, which began in 1932, served to further establish and unify the curricular structure of engineering programs. In 1940, 1960, and 1976, accredited engineering schools in the United States numbered 125, 159, and 234, respectively (Grayson, 1980).

Predictably, the growth of engineering education at black colleges followed a more modest progression. Howard University began offering engineering in 1914 followed by North Carolina A&T in 1920 (Gibbs, 1952). Though all but two of the white land-grant colleges offered engineering by 1928, the black land-grant colleges generally lacked the resources and facilities to do so (Craig, 1992). Eventually, Tennessee State and Tuskegee established engineering programs in 1949; however, by 1963, of the six black colleges with schools of engineering, Howard—having earned national accreditation for electrical and civil engineering in 1936—still operated the only accredited programs (ABET [Accreditation Board for Engineering and Technology], n.d.; Gibbs, 1952; McGrath, 1965).

Despite the steady demand for qualified engineers throughout the twentieth century, "no serious attempts [were] made to develop and utilize the scientific and technical talents of racial and ethnic minorities" (Wilburn, 1974, p. 1148). With the enactment of affirmative action policies that linked federal funding to minority representation, however, an "EEO-induced" rationale for increasing African American participation in engineering emerged (Wilburn, 1974, p. 1148). Eventually, the basis for this call for broader participation in the STEM fields took on a more culturally progressive tone, acknowledging the country's increasing diversity and the need to improve the extent to which human capital is developed to remain competitive globally. This modern case for diversity in engineering is articulated in numerous recent reports (National Action Council for Minorities in Engineering, 2008; Perna and others, 2007; National Science Foundation, 2006, 2007; Southern Education Foundation, 2005).

In the past thirty years, African American representation among engineering bachelor's degree recipients has increased steadily, though moderately, from 3.3 percent in 1977 to 4.6 percent in 2007, with a peak of 5.1 percent in 2001 (National Science Foundation, 2009). Even though African Americans remain significantly underrepresented, HBCUs have and continue to play a critical role in producing black engineers. Nine of the top twenty institutions conferring engineering baccalaureate degrees to African Americans are HBCUs. Similarly, although black colleges make up only 3 percent of all institutions of higher education, during the period from 1997 to 2006 they accounted for 20.1 to 29.4 percent of blacks who earned baccalaureate degrees in engineering. Yet perhaps the most telling aspect of the role of HBCUs in advancing engineering education is revealed in Exhibit 3, which shows that all of the top ten baccalaureate institutions of black science and engineering doctorate recipients from 2002 to 2006 were historically black colleges.

As of 2008, sixteen HBCUs had nationally accredited engineering programs that spanned the disciplinary gamut (ABET, n.d.). Indeed, attempts to diversify the face of engineering must include thoughtful analysis of these institutions that have already demonstrated consistent gains in this area. Similarly, the record of partnerships between HBCUs and HWIs that also focus on engineering such as the dual-degree program between the Atlanta University Center and the College of Engineering at Georgia Institute of Technology should be studied and built upon as another approach to expanding the engineering talent pool.

Accreditation

In recent years, the debate about the relevance of HBCUs has often been fueled by controversial, seemingly ubiquitous problems related to accreditation. Since

EXHIBIT 3
Top Baccalaureate Institutions of Black Science and Engineering Doctorate Recipients, 2002–2006

Baccalaureate Institution	Number of Doctorates
Howard University	102
Spelman College	78
Florida A&M University	70
Hampton University	67
Morehouse College	51
Morgan State University	43
Tuskegee University	43
North Carolina A&T State University	42
Southern University A&M College at Baton Rouge	42
Xavier University	40
University of Maryland at College Park	37
Harvard University	35

Source: Adapted from National Science Foundation, 2007.

1996, at least eleven HBCUs have experienced accreditation reprimands or rescindments (Gasman and others, 2007). As a measure of quality tied to federal and state funding as well as membership in the United Negro College Fund, for example, once a troubled institution becomes embroiled in an accreditation quandary, full recovery is difficult to near impossible.

Most HBCUs fall under the jurisdiction of the Southern Association of Colleges and Schools (SACS). Since 1989, HBCUs—13 percent of the SACS institutional membership—have accounted for nearly half of the SACS accreditation rescindments (Gasman and others, 2007). Problems with accreditation generally stem from financial difficulties. For example, in 2002, after mounting a $23 million deficit and purportedly using federal financial aid pay down bills, Morris Brown College lost its accreditation (Gasman and others, 2007). Accrediting agencies, however, do incorporate a variety of aspects in assessing institutional quality (for example, student enrollment, campus infrastructure, and library holdings).

As noted, without accreditation institutions are ineligible for state and federal funding and thus unable to distribute student aid. This situation leads to inevitable enrollment declines and the loss of tuition revenues, drawing the institution into further decline. An unusual example is Bennett College, which under the new leadership of former Spelman president Johnnetta B. Cole, was able to recover from its probationary status. Though Bennett certainly represents the exception rather than the rule with regard to accreditation comebacks, its situation highlights the importance of institutional leadership in this area. To this point, the Southern Education Fund in 2004 established an HBCU leadership development program to "help institutions secure their accreditation status" (Gasman and others, 2007, p. 71).

Whether training engineers, teachers, veterinarians, medical doctors, or journalists, HBCUs have demonstrated an impressive degree of adaptability and resiliency over time with respect to their curricular offerings, despite an often unfavorable, sometimes hostile historical backdrop. In an era of increased accountability, broader student choice, shifting market demands, and persistent questions about their relevance in the contemporary context, however, the curricular leanings and related performance of HBCUs have a heightened—arguably make-or-break—importance. In that sense, rigorous studies of successful, mission-critical programs like Xavier's premedical program, North Carolina A&T's engineering program, and Florida A&M's business program, to name a few, are increasingly warranted. Scholars must qualify and quantify the best practices of such programs, not only to garner support for them and their respective institutions but also to enhance the curricula and benefit students at other colleges and universities—historically both black and white.

Conclusion and Thoughts About the Future

H ISTORICALLY BLACK COLLEGES AND UNIVERSITIES were born out of our nation's troubled and violent history of racism. These institutions are the product of blacks' and whites' working together, albeit often for different and conflicting reasons, to educate African Americans. HBCUs have been shaped by both our achievements as a society and the aspects of our country that reside in its underbelly. Despite critics and adamant opponents to their very existence and with the help of dedicated supporters, HBCUs have survived for decades, often providing an education to those students that other colleges and universities ignore. These institutions have always opened their doors to students, faculty, and staff of all racial and ethnic backgrounds. They have never been segregated in the way that their historically white counterparts have and instead reflect the diversity of our nation.

We hope that this book, which provides an overview of HBCUs as well as the research that has been conducted on them thus far, serves as a starting point for additional research and as a testimony to the impact that HBCUs have had and can have in the future. These institutions are not perfect in the same way that none of our colleges and universities are perfect. But they are worth investing in, financially and intellectually. There is room for growth and improvement if we take seriously the education of marginalized groups; increasing research in this area will only add to the sustainability of HBCUs. Asking hard questions and digging deep for the answers is essential to their future. Scholars must be cognizant and respectful of HBCUs' unique histories when conducting research, but they must not fear being critical when necessary as constructive feedback is the pathway to institutional strength, positive changes, and the ability to thrive.

Despite an increase in research in recent years, much remains to learn about HBCUs, especially in the area of student experiences and the impact of an HBCU education. A considerable void remains in what we know about HBCU students in terms of college choice, experiences, achievement, and labor market outcomes. More robust research is needed in this anti–affirmative action, postracial era to understand how African Americans and other students experience HBCUs while earning their postsecondary credentials. Additional research exploring these issues should provide information relevant to individual institutions, regions, states, and the federal government.

In a highly competitive higher education marketplace, understanding and optimizing recruitment remains a crucial strategic area for HBCUs. More research is needed related to the college choice process for black and nonblack prospective HBCU students. How do students at various academic levels come to learn about, apply to, and enroll in HBCUs? What messages or images are shaping students' perspectives about these institutions?

The leadership at HBCUs is changing. Many younger leaders with arguably different approaches from their predecessors are taking the reins of these institutions. As this transition takes place, scholars need to examine the leadership of these individuals. Who has influenced their leadership approach? What are their priorities for HBCUs? How will they respond to some of the criticism around HBCUs, including low graduation rates, lack of steady financial management, and poor alumni engagement? How will their leadership approach affect the role of faculty and faculty governance? As noted in this text, the majority of the research related to HBCU presidents is historical in nature, and ample room exists for exploration of contemporary leaders.

HBCUs have been affected by policies at the federal, state, and local levels, and future research should address these arenas. Continued attention to critical policy research that juxtaposes HBCU gains and losses beyond just financial is important. The role of these policies in shaping the college-going population for specific states may be of particular importance as attention to the primary-to-college pipeline increases and disparities in many of the poorer southern states are addressed. Public HBCUs may have an especially important role in this realm. The existing literature is also limited when it comes to exploring the outcomes of federal policies such as the Title III Strengthening Historically Black Colleges and Universities Program. The benefits and drawbacks of direct federal investment in these institutions must be clarified.

Research on the different governance structures at HBCUs from their inception to present day should also be undertaken, as governance structures at both public and private institutions across the nation inform higher education forecasting, leadership, institutional mission, and allocations. Particular attention to the role of two-year HBCUs should also be considered, especially in relationship to four-year HBCUs.

To meet changing global market demands that call for an increasingly technical workforce, research on curricula at HBCUs should focus on how and in what ways HBCUs are best able to respond. Whether reviving their teacher education traditions to improve the dismal representation of African Americans among the ranks of K–12 science and mathematics teachers or designing more dual-degree partnerships with HWIs to provide a sound foundation for future engineers and computer scientists, what HBCUs do well relative to curricula and pedagogy must be uncovered and explored. Bringing this aspect of HBCUs to the fore and identifying potential niches could help them assert their rightful place in American higher education as well as serve as a model for more purposeful curriculum and program design at other institutions that seek to develop a diverse student constituency.

Of grave importance is research related to fundraising. Myriad questions have been left unanswered. As HBCU students become alumni, how can HBCUs more effectively tap them as advocates and donors? What are other ways in which HBCUs have engaged or can engage their alumni before they become alumni to strengthen the institution? How might HBCUs take advantage of contemporary tools like social networking to garner alumni support? These questions among others should be the focus of research.

Overall, new scholars have ample room to boost the quality and quantity of research related to HBCUs. But for these new scholars to succeed, it is vital that current faculty members support, mentor, and motivate them to pursue research related to HBCUs and African American higher education. Established scholars must see these institutions as a viable topic of study in academe instead of telling young researchers to shy away from them out of fear that research-ing something related to race or "nonelite" institutions will harm their careers. As the demographics of the nation change, HBCUs and other minority-serving institutions will become even more important to the future of the country as they are equipped with the skills and talent to educate a diverse stu-dent population. Research on HBCUs in the coming years will be even more crucial to the future of our nation.

Appendix: Historically Black Colleges and Universities

Alabama

Alabama A&M University

Alabama State University

Bishop State Community College

Concordia College–Selma

Gadsden State Community College, Valley Street

J.F. Drake State Technical College

Lawson State Community College

Miles College

Oakwood University

Selma University

Shelton State Community College, C.A. Fredd Campus

Stillman College

Talladega College

Trenholm State Technical College

Tuskegee University

Arkansas

Arkansas Baptist College

Philander Smith College

Shorter College

University of Arkansas at Pine Bluff

Delaware

Delaware State University

District of Columbia

Howard University

University of the District of Columbia

Florida

Bethune-Cookman College

Edward Waters College

Florida A&M University

Florida Memorial University

Georgia

Albany State University

Clark Atlanta University

Fort Valley State University

Interdenominational Theological Center

Morehouse College
Morehouse School of Medicine
Morris Brown College
Paine College
Savannah State University
Spelman College

Kentucky
Kentucky State University

Louisiana
Dillard University of Louisiana
Grambling State University
Southern University A&M College
Southern University at New Orleans
Southern University at Shreveport
Xavier University

Maryland
Bowie State University
Coppin State College
Morgan State University
University of Maryland, Eastern
  Shore

Michigan
Lewis College of Business

Mississippi
Alcorn State University

Coahoma Community College
Hinds Community College, Utica
Jackson State University
Mississippi Valley State University
Rust College
Tougaloo College

Missouri
Harris-Stowe State University
Lincoln University

North Carolina
Barber-Scotia College
Bennett College
Elizabeth City State University
Fayetteville State University
Johnson C. Smith University
Livingstone College
North Carolina A&T State
  University
North Carolina Central University
St. Augustine's College
Shaw University
Winston-Salem State University

Ohio
Central State University
Wilberforce University

Oklahoma
Langston University

Pennsylvania

Cheyney University of Pennsylvania

Lincoln University

South Carolina

Allen University

Benedict College

Claflin University

Clinton Junior College

Denmark Technical College

Morris College

South Carolina State University

Voorhees College

Tennessee

Fisk University

Knoxville College

Lane College

Lemoyne-Owen College

Meharry Medical College

Tennessee State University

Texas

Huston-Tillotson University

Jarvis Christian College

Paul Quinn College

Prairie View A&M University

St. Philip's College

Southwestern Christian College

Texas College

Texas Southern University

Wiley College

U.S. Virgin Islands

University of the Virgin Islands

Virginia

Hampton University

Norfolk State University

Saint Paul's College

Virginia State University

Virginia Union University

Virginia University of Lynchburg

West Virginia

Bluefield State College

West Virginia State University

References

ABET Accredited programs. (n.d.). Retrieved June 24, 2009, from http://www.abet.org.

Adams, F. (1986). Why *Brown v. Board of Education* and affirmative action can save historically black colleges and universities. *Alabama Law Review*, *47*(2), 481–511.

Agesa, J., Granger, M., and Price, G. N. (2002). Swimming upstream? The relative research productivity of economists at black colleges. *Review of Black Political Economy*, *29*(3), 71–93.

Allen, W. R. (1992). The color of success: African American college student outcomes at predominantly white and historically black public colleges and universities. *Harvard Educational Review*, *62*, 26–44.

Allen, W. R., and Haniff, N. Z. (1991). Race, gender, and academic performance in U.S. higher education. In W. R. Allen, E. G. Epps, and N. Z. Haniff (Eds.), *College in black and white* (pp. 95–109). Albany: State University of New York Press.

Allen, W. R., and Jewell, J. O. (2002). A backward glance forward: Past, present and future perspectives on historically black colleges and universities. *Review of Higher Education*, *25*(3), 241–261.

American Association of University Professors. (1995, January–February). The historically black colleges and universities: A future in the balance. *Academe*, *81*(1), 49–58.

Anderson, J. D. (1988). *The education of blacks in the south, 1860–1935*. Chapel Hill: University of North Carolina Press.

Ashley, D. (2001, July 5). Capital campaigns. *Black Issues in Higher Education*, *18*(10), 18–25.

Baxter, F. V. (1982). The affirmative duty to desegregate institutions of higher education: Defining the role of the traditionally black college. *Journal of Law & Education*, *11*(1), 1–40.

Benjamin, L. (2004). *Dreaming no small dreams: William R. Harvey's visionary leadership*. Arlington, VA: Tapestry Press.

Berger, J. B., and Milem, J. F. (2000). Exploring the impact of historically black colleges in promoting the development of undergraduates' self-concept. *Journal of College Student Development*, *41*(4), 381–394.

Betsey, C. (2007). Faculty research productivity: Institutional and personal determinants of faculty publications. *Review of Black Political Economy, 34*(1/2), 53–85.

Billingsley, A. (1982). Building strong faculties in black colleges. *Journal of Negro Education, 51*(1), 4–15.

Blake, A. C. (2006). The experiences and adjustment problems of Africans at a historically black institution. *College Student Journal, 40*(4), 808–813.

Bonner, F. B. (2001). Addressing gender issues in the historically black colleges and universities community: A challenge and call to action. *Journal of Negro Education, 70*(3), 176–191.

Bonous-Hammarth, M., and Boatsman, K. (1996). Satisfaction guaranteed? Predicting academic and social outcomes for African American college students. Paper presented at the Annual Conference of the American Educational Research Association, New York.

Boone, P. R. (2003). When the "amen corner" comes to class: An examination of the pedagogical and cultural impact of call-response communication in the black college classroom. *Communication Education, 52*(3/4), 212–229.

Boren, S., and others. (1987). The higher education amendments of 1986 (P.L. 99–498): A summary of provisions. 87–187 EPW. Washington, DC: Congressional Research Service.

Bowles, F., and DeCosta, F. (1971). *Between two worlds: A profile of Negro higher education.* New York: Carnegie Foundation for the Advancement of Teaching.

Brady, K., Eatman, T., and Parker, L. (2000). To have or not to have? A preliminary analysis of higher education funding disparities in the post-*Ayers* v. *Fordice* era: Evidence from critical race theory. *Journal of Education Finance, 25*(3), 297–322.

Brazziel, W. F. (1960). Curriculum choice in the Negro college. *Journal of Negro Education, 29*(2), 201–207.

Brooks, F. E. (2004). Legal and policy issues: Removing the residue of past segregation in higher education. *Journal of Negro Education, 73*(3), 350–364.

Brown, I. C. (1942). The national survey of Negro higher education and postwar reconstruction: The place of the Negro college in Negro life. *Journal of Negro Education, 11*(3), 375–381.

Brown, M. C., II. (1998). African American college student retention and the ecological psychology of historically black colleges. *National Association of Student Affairs Professionals Journal, 1*(1), 50–66.

Brown, M. C., II. (1999). *The quest to define collegiate desegregation: Black colleges, Title VI compliance, and post-Adams litigation.* Westport, CT: Bergin & Garvey.

Brown, M. C., II. (2001). Collegiate desegregation and the public black college: A new policy mandate. *Journal of Higher Education, 72*(1), 46–62.

Brown, M. C., II, Donahoo, S., and Bertrand, R. D. (2001). The black college and the quest for educational opportunity. *Urban Education, 36*(5), 553–571.

Brown, M. C., II, and Freeman, K. (Eds.). (2004). *Black colleges: New perspectives on policy and practice.* Westport, CT: Praeger.

Brown, T. L., Parks, G. S., and Phillips, C. M. (Eds.). (2005). *African American fraternities and sororities: The legacy and the vision.* Lexington: University of Kentucky Press.

Byrd, A. (1990). (Ed.). *Philanthropy and the black church*. Washington, DC: Council on Foundations.

Carter, L. (1998). *Walking integrity: Benjamin Elijah Mays, mentor to Martin Luther King, Jr.* Mercer, GA: Mercer University Press.

Chavous, T. M., Harris, A., Rivas, D., Helaire, L., and Green, L. (2004). Racial stereotypes and gender in context: African Americans at predominantly black and predominantly white colleges. *Sex Roles, 51*(1/2), 1–16.

Chism, M., and Satcher, J. (1998). African-American students' perceptions toward faculty at historically black colleges. *College Student Journal, 32*(2), 315–320.

Chung, C., and Carlon, A. (2006). HIV on historically black colleges and universities (HBCU): A study of five campuses in Texas, Oklahoma, and Louisiana. *College Student Journal, 40*(1), 25–34.

Christy, R. D., and Williamson, L. (1992). *A century of service: Land-grant colleges and universities, 1890–1990*. New Brunswick, NJ: Transaction Publishers.

Closson, R. B., and Henry, W. J. (2008). The social adjustment of undergraduate white students in the minority on an historically black college campus. *Journal of College Student Development, 49*(6), 517–534.

Cokley, K. O. (2001). Gender differences among African American students in the impact of racial identity on academic psychosocial development. *Journal of College Student Development, 42*, 480–487.

Cokley, K. O. (2005). Racial(ized) identity, ethnic identity, and Afrocentric values: Conceptual and methodological challenges in understanding African American identity. *Journal of Counseling Psychology, 52*(4), 517–526.

Cole, B. (1977). Appropriation politics and black schools: Howard University in the U.S. Congress, 1879–1928. *Journal of Negro Education, 46*(1), 7–23.

Cole, W. M. (2006). Accrediting culture: An analysis of tribal and historically black college curricula. *Sociology of Education, 79*(4), 355–387.

Conrad, C. F., Brier, E. M., and Braxton, J. M. (1997). Factors contributing to the matriculation of white students in public HBCUs. *Journal for a Just and Caring Education, 3*(1), 37–62.

Constantine, J. M. (1995). The effect of attending historically black colleges and universities on future wages of black students. *Industrial and Labor Relations Review, 48*(3), 531–546.

Cooper, J. E., Massey, D., and Graham, A. (2006). Being "Dixie" at a historically black university: A white faculty member's exploration of whiteness through the narratives of two black faculty members. *Negro Educational Review, 57*(1–2), 117–135.

Cooperative State Research, Education, and Extension Service. (n.d.). 1890 land-grant institutions. Retrieved June 3, 2009, from http://www.csrees.usda.gov/qlinks/partners/state_partners.html.

Craig, L. A. (1991). Constrained resource allocation and the investment in the education of Black Americans: The 1890 land-grant colleges. *Agricultural History, 65*(2), 73–84.

Craig, L. A. (1992). "Raising among themselves": Black educational advancement and the Morrill Act of 1890. *Agriculture and Human Values, 9*(1), 31–37.

Cross, P. H., and Astin, H. (1981). Factors affecting black students' persistence in college. In G. Thomas (Ed.), *Black Students in Higher Education: Conditions and Experiences in the 1970's* (pp. 76–90). Westport, CT: Greenwood.

Daniel, W. G., and Daniel, R. P. (1946). The curriculum of the Negro college. *Journal of Educational Sociology, 19*(8), 496–502.

Davis, L. (1998). *Clashing of the soul: John Hope and the dilemma of African American leadership and black higher education in the early twentieth century.* Athens: University of Georgia Press.

DeSousa, D. J., and Kuh, G. D. (1996). Does institutional racial composition make a difference in what black students gain from college? *Journal of College Student Development, 37*(3), 257–267.

Dreher, G. F., and Chargois, J. A. (1998). Gender, mentoring experiences, and salary attainment among graduates of a historically black university. *Journal of Vocational Behavior, 53*(3), 401–416.

Drewry, H. N., and Doermann, H. (2001). *Stand and prosper: Private black colleges and their students.* Princeton, NJ: Princeton University Press.

Drezner, N. (2008). Cultivating a culture of giving: An exploration of institutional strategies to enhance African American young alumni giving. Ph.D. dissertation, University of Pennsylvania, Philadelphia.

Du Bois, W.E.B. (1903/2005). *The souls of black folks.* London: Paradigm.

Edgecomb, G. S. (1993). *From swastika to Jim Crow: Refugee scholars at black colleges.* Malabar, FL: Krieger.

Ehrenberg, R. G., and Rothstein, D. S. (1994). Do historically black institutions of higher education confer unique advantages on black students? An initial analysis. In R. G. Ehrenberg (Ed.), *Choices and consequences: Contemporary policy issues in education* (pp. 89–137). Ithaca, NY: ILR Press.

Engs, R. (1999). *Educating the disfranchised and disinherited: Samuel Chapman Armstrong and Hampton Institute.* Knoxville: University of Tennessee Press.

Fairclough, A. (2007). *A class of their own: Black teachers in the segregated South.* Cambridge, MA: Harvard University Press.

Fairfax, J. E. (1995, Summer). Black philanthropy: Its heritage and its future. *New Directions for Philanthropic Fundraising, 8,* 9–21.

Farazzo, D. E., and Stevens, A. (2004). Topography of learning style preferences of undergraduate students in industrial technology and engineering programs at historically black and predominately white institutions. *Journal of Industrial Teacher Education, 41*(3), 20–33.

Ferguson, Y. O., Quinn, S. C., Eng, E., and Sandelowski, M. (2006). The gender ratio imbalance and its relationship to risk of HIV/AIDS among African American women at historically black colleges and universities. *AIDS Care, 18*(4), 323–331.

Fleming, J. (1984). *Blacks in college: A comparative study of students' success in black and white institutions.* San Francisco: Jossey-Bass.

Flowers, L. A. (2002). The impact of college racial composition on African American students' academic and social gains: Additional evidence. *Journal of College Student Development, 43*(3), 403–410.

Foster, L. (2001). The not-so-invisible professors: White faculty at the black college. *Urban Education, 36*(5), 611–629.

Foster, L., Guyden, J. A., and Miller, A. L. (1999). *Affirmed action: Essays on the academic and social lives of white faculty members at historically black colleges and universities.* Lanham, MD: Rowman & Littlefield.

Frazier, E. F. (1957). *Black bourgeoisie.* New York: Free Press.

Frazier, E. F. (1963). *The Negro church in America.* New York: Schocken Books.

Frazier, E. F. (1977). *Black bourgeoisie.* New York: Free Press Paperbacks, Simon & Schuster.

Freeman, K. (1999). HBCUs or PWIs? African American high school students' consideration of higher education institution types. *Review of Higher Education, 23*(1), 91–106.

Freeman, K. (2005). African American college choice and the influence of family and school. Albany, NY: SUNY Press.

Freeman, K., and Thomas, G. E. (2002). Black colleges and college choice: Characteristics of students who choose HBCUs. *Review of Higher Education, 25*(3), 349–358.

Fries-Britt, S. L., and Turner, B. (2002). Uneven stories: Successful black collegians at a black and a white campus. *Review of Higher Education, 25*(3), 315–330.

Fryer, R. G., and Greenston, M. (2007). *The causes and consequences of attending historically black colleges and universities.* Working Paper 13036. Cambridge, MA: National Bureau of Economic Research.

Gabbidon, S. L., and others. (2008). The consumer racial profiling experiences of black students at historically black colleges and universities: An exploratory study. *Journal of Criminal Justice, 36*(4), 354–361.

Garrett, R. U. (2006). Effects of mentoring on the quality of the doctoral experience at historically black colleges and universities: Results of groundwork investigation. *Race, Gender & Class, 13*(3/4), 311–328.

Gasman, M. (1999). Scylla and Charybdis: Navigating the waters of academic freedom at Fisk University during Charles S. Johnson's administration (1946–1956). *American Educational Research Journal, 36*(4), 739–758.

Gasman, M. (2001a). Charles S. Johnson and Johnnetta Cole: Successful role models for fundraising at historically black colleges and universities. *CASE International Journal of Educational Advancement, 1*(3), 237–252.

Gasman, M. (2001b). Passport to the front of the bus: The impact of Fisk University's international program on race relations in Nashville, Tennessee. *49th Parallel: The International Journal of North American Studies, 7.* Retrieved January 12, 2006, from http://www.49thparallel.bham.ac.uk/back/issue7/gasman.htm.

Gasman, M. (2001c). The president as ethical role model: Instilling an ethic of leadership at Fisk University during the 1950s. *Journal of College and Character, 2.* Retrieved January 17, 2006, from http://www.collegevalues.org/articles.cfm?a=1andid=510.

Gasman, M. (2004). Rhetoric vs. reality: The fundraising messages of the United Negro College Fund in the immediate aftermath of the *Brown* decision. *History of Education Quarterly, 44*(1), 70–94.

Gasman, M. (2007a). Historically black colleges and universities and the issue of gender. In B. J. Bank, S. Delamont, and C. Marshall (Eds.), *Gender and Education* (pp. 35–50). Westport, CT: Greenwood Publishing.

Gasman, M. (2007b). Swept under the rug? A historiography of gender and black colleges. *American Educational Research Journal, 44*(4), 760–805.

Gasman, M. (2008a). *Envisioning black colleges: A history of the United Negro College Fund.* Baltimore: Johns Hopkins University Press.

Gasman, M. (2008b). *Minority serving institutions: The pathway to success for students of color.* Indianapolis: Lumina Foundation for Education.

Gasman, M., and Anderson-Thompkins, S. (2003). *Fundraising from Black Colleges Alumni: Successful Strategies for Supporting Alma Mater.* Washington, D.C.: Council for the Advancement and Support of Education.

Gasman, M., Baez, B., and Turner, C. S. (Eds.). (2008). *Understanding minority serving institutions.* Albany, NY: SUNY Press.

Gasman, M., and Drezner, N. (2008). White corporate philanthropy and its support of private black colleges in the 1960s and 70s. *International Journal of Educational Advancement, 8*(2), 79–92.

Gasman, M., and Drezner, N. (2009a). Fundraising during the midst of the civil rights movement: The case of Hampton Institute. *Nonprofit Sector and Voluntary Quarterly Online.* http://nvs.sagepub.com/cgi/rapidpdf/0899764009333051v1.

Gasman, M., and Drezner, N. (2009b). A maverick in the field: Fundraising for change in the black college community during the 1970s. *History of Education Quarterly, 49*(4), 465–500.

Gasman, M., and others. (2007). Historically Black Colleges and Universities: Recent Trends, *Academe, 93*(1), 69–77.

Gasman, M., and Sedgwick, K. (2005). *Uplifting a people: African American philanthropy and education.* New York: Peter Lang.

Geiger, S. M. (2007). *Understanding gender at public historically black colleges and universities.* Washington, DC: Thurgood Marshall Fund.

Gibbs, W. T. (1952). Engineering education in Negro land-grant colleges. *Journal of Negro Education, 21*(4), 546–550.

Gilpin, P. J., and Gasman, M. (2003). *Charles S. Johnson: Leadership behind the veil in the age of Jim Crow.* Albany, NY: SUNY Press.

Goodson, M. G. (Ed.). (1991). *Chronicles of faith: The autobiography of Frederick D. Patterson.* Tuscaloosa: University of Alabama Press.

Grayson, L. P. (1980). A brief history of engineering education in the United States. *IEEE Transactions on Aerospace and Electronic Systems, AES-16*(3), 373–391.

Green, P. (2004). Other things being equal: Federal aid and the politics of equal opportunity for historically black colleges and universities. In M. C. Brown, II, and K. Freeman (Eds.), *Black colleges: New perspectives on policy and practice* (pp. 65–85). Westport, CT: Praeger.

Gurin, P., and Epps, E. (1975). *Black consciousness, identity, and achievement: A study of students in historically black colleges.* New York: Wiley.

Guy-Sheftall, B. (2006). Shared governance, junior faculty, and HBCUs. *Academe, 92*(6), 30–34.

Hale, F. W., Jr. (Ed.). (2006). *How black colleges empower black students: Lessons from higher education.* Sterling, SC: Stylus.

Hall, B., and Closson, R. B. (2005). When the majority is the minority: White graduate students' social adjustment at a historically black university. *Journal of College Student Development, 46*(1), 28–42.

Hall-Russell, C. (1999). *Rising to the call: Evolving philanthropic trends in the African American megachurch.* Indianapolis: Center on Philanthropy.

Hall-Russell, C., and Kasberg, R. H. (1997). *African American traditions of giving and serving: A midwest perspective.* Indianapolis: Indiana University Center on Philanthropy.

Harlan, L. R. (Ed.). (1974). *The Booker T. Washington papers.* (Vol. 3). Urbana: University of Illinois Press.

Harley, D. A. (2001). Desegregation at HBCUs: Removing barriers and implementing strategies. *Negro Educational Review, 52*(4), 151–164.

Harley, D. A., Tennessee, W., Alston, J. R., and Wilson, T. (2000). HBCUs' desegregation challenge: Strategies for recruiting traditional majority students' representation. *Rehabilitation Education, 14*(4), 410–423.

Harper, S. R., Carini, R. M., Bridges, B. K., and Hayek, J. C. (2004). Gender differences in student engagement among African American undergraduates at historically black colleges and universities. *Journal of College Student Development, 45*(3), 271–284.

Harris, J. J., III, Figgures, C., and Carter, D. G. (1975). A historical perspective of the emergence of higher education in black colleges. *Journal of Black Studies, 6*(1), 55–68.

Harvey, W. B., and Williams, L. E. (1989). Historically black colleges: Models for increasing minority representation. *Education and Urban Society, 1*(3), 328–340.

Hill, S. T. (1984). *The Traditionally Black Institutions of Higher Education, 1860 to 1982.* Washington, DC: U.S. Government Printing Office.

Holloman, D., Gasman, M., and Anderson-Thompkins, S. (2003). Motivations for philanthropic giving in the African American church: Implications for black college fundraising. *Journal of Research on Christian Education, 12*(2), 137–169.

Hossler, D., and Gallagher, K. S. (1987). Studying student college choice: A three-phase model and the implications for policymakers. *College and University, 62*(3), 207–221.

Humphries, F. S. (1991). 1890 land-grant institutions: Their struggle for survival and equality. *Agricultural History, 65*(2), 3–11.

Jackson, C. L., and Nunn, E. F. (2003). *Historically black colleges and universities: A reference handbook.* Contemporary Education Issues. Santa Barbara: ABC-CLIO.

Jackson, J.F.L., Snowden, M., and Eckes, S. (2002). *Fordice* as a window of opportunity: The case for maintaining historically black colleges and universities (HBCUs) as predominantly black institutions. *West's Education Law Reporter, 1,* 1–19.

Jaffe, A. J., Adams, W., and Meyers, S. G. (1968). *Negro higher education in the 1960s.* New York: Praeger.

Jencks, C., and Riesman, D. (1967). The American Negro college. *Harvard Educational Review, 37*(1), 3–60.

Jenkins, M. D. (1942). The national survey of Negro higher education and postwar reconstruction: The resources of Negro higher education. *Journal of Negro Education, 11*(3), 382–390.

Jenkins, M. D. (1946). Enrollment in Negro colleges and universities, 1945–46. *Journal of Negro Education, 15*(2), 231–239.

Jenkins, M. D. (1947). Graduate work in Negro institutions of higher education. *Journal of Negro Education, 18*(6), 300–306.

Jenkins, M. D. (1958). The future of the desegregated Negro college: A critical summary. *Journal of Negro Education, 27*(3), 419–429.

Jewell, J. (2002). To set an example: The tradition of diversity at historically black colleges and universities. *Urban Education, 37*(1), 7–21.

Johnson, B. J. (2001). Faculty socialization: Lessons learned from urban black colleges. *Urban Education, 36*(5), 630–647.

Johnson, B. J., and Harvey, W. (2002). The socialization of black college faculty: Implications for policy and practice. *Review of Higher Education, 25*(3), 297–314.

Kim, M. M. (2002). Historically black vs. white institutions: Academic development among black students. *Review of Higher Education, 25*(4), 385–407.

Kim, M. M., and Conrad, C. F. (2006). The impact of historically black colleges and universities on the academic success of African American students. *Research in Higher Education, 47*(4), 399–427.

Kimbrough, R. M., Molock, S. D., and Walton, K. (1996). Perception of social support, acculturation, depression, and suicidal ideation among African American college students at predominantly black and predominantly white universities. *Journal of Negro Education, 65*(3), 295–307.

Kimbrough, W. (2003). *Black Greek 101.* Teaneck, NJ: Fairleigh Dickinson University Press.

Kimbrough, W., and Harper, S. R. (2006). African American men at historically black colleges and universities: Different environments, similar challenges. In M. L. Cuyjet (Ed.), *African American men in college* (pp. 189–209). San Francisco: Jossey-Bass.

Kujovich, G. (1993, Winter). Public black colleges: The long history of unequal funding. *Journal of Blacks in Higher Education, 2,* 73–82.

Ladson, G. M., Lin, J., Flores, A., and Magrane, D. (2006). An assessment of cultural competence of first- and second-year medical students at a historically diverse medical school. *American Journal of Obstetrics & Gynecology, 195*(5), 1457–1462.

Lang, M. (1986). Black student retention at black colleges and universities: Problems, issues, and alternatives. *Western Journal of Black Studies, 10*(2), 48–53.

Laws, M. A., Holliday, R. C., and Huang, C. J. (2007). Prevalence and social norms associated with cigarette smoking among college students attending historically black colleges and universities. *American Journal of Health Studies, 22*(2), 96–104.

Laws, M. A., and others. (2006). Cigarette smoking among college students attending a historically black college and university. *Journal of Health Care for the Poor and Underserved, 17*(1), 143–156.

Lent, R.W., and others. (2005). Social cognitive predictors of academic interests and goals in engineering: Utility for women and students at historically black universities. *Journal of Counseling Psychology, 52*(1), 84–92.

Lieberman, R. C. (1994). The Freedmen's Bureau and the politics of institutional structure. *Social Science History, 18*(3), 405–437.

Lincoln, C. E. (1974). *The black church since Frazier.* New York: Schocken Books.

Logan, R. (1969). *Howard University: The first hundred years 1867–1967.* New York: New York University Press.

Lott, J. L., II. (2008). Racial identity and black students' perceptions of community outreach: Implications for bonding social capital. *Journal of Negro Education, 77*(1), 3–14.

Manley, A. (1995). *Legacy continues: The Manley years at Spelman College, 1953–1976.* New York: University Press of America.

Mays, B. (2003). *Born to rebel.* Athens: University of Georgia.

Mbajekwe, C. O. (2006). *Future of historically black colleges and universities: Ten presidents speak out.* Jefferson, NC: McFarland.

McDonough, P. M., Antonio, A. L., and Trent, J. W. (1997). Black students, black colleges: An African American college choice model. *Journal for a Just and Caring Education, 3*(1), 9–36.

McGrath, E. J. (1965). *The predominantly Negro colleges and universities in transition.* New York: Teachers College, Columbia University.

McKinney, R. (1997). *Mordecai, the man and his message: The story of Mordecai Wyatt Johnson.* Washington, DC: Howard University Press.

McNeal, G. J. (2003, January–February). African American nurse faculty satisfaction and scholarly productivity at predominantly white and historically black colleges and universities. *Association of Black Nursing Faculty Journal, 14*(1), 4–12.

Measuring Up. (2008). San Jose: National Center for Postsecondary Education.

Meier, A. (1992). *A white scholar in the black community, 1945–1965.* Amherst: University of Massachusetts Press.

Mercer, C. (2008). *Title III and Title V of the Higher Education Act: Background and reauthorization issues,* CRS Report No. RL31647. Washington, DC: Congressional Research Service.

Milem, J., and Astin, H. (1993). The changing composition of faculty: What does it really mean for diversity? *Change, 25*(2), 21–27.

Minor, J. T. (2005). Faculty governance at historically black colleges and universities. *Academe, 91*(3), 34–37.

Minor, J. T. (2008). *Contemporary HBCUs: Considering institutional capacity and state priorities.* Research report. East Lansing: College of Education, Michigan State University.

Mumper, M., and Freeman, M. L. (2005). The causes and consequences of public college tuition inflation. In J. C. Smart (Ed.). *Higher education: A handbook of theory and research* (pp. 307–362). New York: Agathon Press.

Myrdal, G. (1944). *An American dilemma.* New York: HarperCollins.

Nasim, A., Roberts, A., Harrell, J. P., and Young, H. (2005). Noncognitive predictors of academic achievement for African Americans across cultural contexts. *Journal of Negro Education, 74*(4), 344–358.

National Action Council for Minorities in Engineering. (2008). *Confronting the "new" American dilemma—underrepresented minorities in engineering: A data-based look at diversity.* White Plains, NY: National Action Council for Minorities in Engineering.

National Science Foundation. (2006). *Investing in America's future: Strategic plan 2006–2011.* NSF 06-48. Arlingon, VA: National Science Foundation.

National Science Foundation. (2007). *Women, minorities, and persons with disabilities in science and engineering.* NSF 07-315. Arlington, VA: National Science Foundation.

National Science Foundation. (2009). *IPEDs completions survey by race, 1977–2007.* Arlington, VA: National Science Foundation. Available at http://webcaspar.nsf.gov.

Nettles, M. T., and Perna, L. W. (1997). *The African American education data book: Preschool through high school education, volume II.* Fairfax, VA: Frederick D. Patterson Research Institute of The College Fund/UNCF.

Nettles, M. T., Perna, L. W., Edelin, K. C., and Robertson, N. (1996). *The College Fund/UNCF statistical report, 1997.* Fairfax, VA: College Fund/UNCF.

Nettles, M. T., Wagener, U., Millett, C., and Killenbeck, A. (1999). Student retention and progression: A special challenge for private historically black colleges and universities. *New Directions for Higher Education, 27*(4). San Francisco: Jossey-Bass.

Nichols, J. C. (2004). Unique characteristics, leadership styles, and management of historically black colleges and universities. *Innovative Higher Education, 28*(3), 219–229.

Nixon, H. L., and Henry, W. J. (1992). White students at the black university: Their experiences regarding acts of racial intolerance. *Equity and Excellence in Education, 25*(2–4), 121–123.

Onkst, D. H. (1998). First a Negro . . . incidentally a veteran: Black World War Two veterans and the GI Bill of Rights in the Deep South, 1944–1948. *Journal of Social History, 31*(3), 517–543.

Outcalt, C. L., and Skewes-Cox, T. E. (2002). Involvement, interaction, and satisfaction: The human environment at HBCUs. *Review of Higher Education, 25*(3), 331–347.

Palmer, R., and Gasman, M. (2008). It takes a village to raise a child: Social capital and academic success at historically black colleges and universities. *Journal of College Student Development, 49*, 52–70.

Palmer, R. T., and Strayhorn, T. L. (2008). Mastering one's own fate: Non-cognitive factors associated with the success of African American males at an HBCU. *NASAP, 11*(1), 126–143.

Parker, M. H. (1954). Educational activities of the Freedmen's Bureau. *Journal of Negro Education, 23*(1), 9–21.

Perna, L. (2001). The contribution of historically black colleges and universities to the preparation of African Americans for faculty careers. *Research in Higher Education, 42*(3), 267–294.

Perna, L. W., and others, (2006). The status of equity for black undergraduates in public higher education in the South. *Research in Higher Education, 47*, 197–228.

Perna, L., and others. (2007, November). *The contribution of HBCUs to the preparation of African American women for STEM careers: A case study.* Paper presented at an annual meeting of the Association for the Study of Higher Education, Louisville, Kentucky.

Perna, L. W., and others. (2009). The contribution of HBCUs to the preparation of African American women for STEM careers: A case study. *Review of Higher Education, 50*(1), 1–50.

Peters, R. J., Jr., and others. (2005). Beliefs and social norms about Ephedra onset and perceived addiction among college male and female athletes. *Substance Use & Misuse, 40*(1), 125–135.

Phillips, I. P. (2002). Shared governance on black college campuses. *Academe, 88*(4), 50–54.

Pressley, C. (Spring, 1995). Financial contributions for the kingdom for the elect: Giving patterns in the Black church. *New Directions for Philanthropic Fundraising, 7*, 91–100.

Price, G. (2007). Would increased National Science Foundation research support to economists at historically Black college and universities increase their research productivity? *Review of Black Political Economy, 34*(1/2), 87–109.

Provasnik, S., Shafer, L. L., and Snyder, T. D. (2004). *Historically black colleges and universities, 1976–2001.* NCES 2004-062. Washington, DC: National Center for Education Statistics.

Reid, R. D. (1967). Curricular changes in colleges and universities for Negroes: Analysis and interpretation of a questionnaire survey. *Journal of Higher Education, 38*(3), 153–160.

Reitzes, D. C., and Elkhanialy, H. (1976). Black physicians and minority group health care: The impact of NMF. *Medical Care, 14*(12), 1052–1060.

Renzulli, L. A., Grant, L., and Kathuria, S. (2006). Race, gender, and the wage gap: Comparing faculty salaries in predominately white and historically black colleges and universities. *Gender & Society, 20*(4), 491–510.

Ricard, R. B., and Brown, M. C., II. (2008). *Ebony towers in higher education: The evolution, mission, and presidency of historically black colleges and universities.* Sterling, SC: Stylus.

Richardson, J. W., and Harris, J. J., III. (2004). *Brown* and historically black colleges and universities (HBCUs): A paradox of desegregation policy. *Journal of Negro Education, 73*(3), 365–378.

Riggins, R. K., McNeal, C., and Herndon, M. K. (2008). The role of spirituality among African American college males attending a historically black university. *College Student Journal, 42*(1), 70–81.

Robbins, R. (1996). *Sidelines activist: Charles S. Johnson and the struggle for civil rights.* Jackson: University of Mississippi Press.

Ross, L. (2001). *Divine nine: The history of African American fraternities and sororities.* New York: Kensington Publishing Corp.

Ross, M. J. (1998). *Success factors of young African American men at a historically black college.* Westport, CT: Praeger.

Savitt, T. L. (2006). *Race and medicine in nineteenth and early twentieth century America.* Kent, OH: Kent State University Press.

Sibulkin, A., and Butler, J. S. (2005). Differences in graduation rates between young black and white college students: Effect of entry into parenthood and historically black universities. *Research in Higher Education, 46*(3), 327–348.

Singh, K., Robinson, A., and Williams-Green, J. (1995). Differences in perceptions of African American women and men faculty and administrators. *Journal of Negro Education, 64*, 401–408.

Smith, G. (1994). *Black educator in the segregated south: Kentucky's Rufus B. Atwood.* Lexington: University of Kentucky Press.

Smith, S. L., and Borgstedt, K. W. (1985). Factors influencing adjustment of white faculty in predominantly black colleges. *Journal of Negro Education, 54*(2), 148–163.

Solorzano, D. G. (1995). The doctorate production and baccalaureate origins of African Americans in the sciences and engineering. *Journal of Negro Education, 64*(1), 15–32.

Southern Education Foundation. (2005). *Igniting potential: Historically black colleges and universities in science, technology, engineering, and mathematics.* Atlanta: Southern Education Foundation.

Stier, W. (1992). Characteristics of physical education faculty in historically black colleges and universities (HBCUs). *Physical Educator, 49*(2), 73–80.

Strayhorn, T. L. (2008). Influences on labor market outcomes of African American college graduates: A national study. *Journal of Higher Education, 79*(1), 28–57.

Tabbye, C., and others. (2004). Racial stereotypes and gender in context: African Americans at predominantly black and predominantly white colleges. *Journal of Research, 51*(1–2), 1–16.

Thelin, J. R. (2004). *A history of American higher education.* Baltimore: Johns Hopkins University Press.

Thomas, G. E., and McPartland, J. (1984). Have college desegregation policies threatened black student enrollment and black colleges? An empirical analysis. *Journal of Negro Education, 53*(4), 389–399.

Thompson, C. J., and Dey, E. L. (1998). Pushed to the margins: Sources of stress for African American college and university faculty. *Journal of Higher Education, 69*(3), 324–345.

Thompson, D. C. (1973). *Private black colleges at the crossroads.* Westport, CT: Greenwood.

Thompson-Robins, M., and others. (2005). Perceptions of partner risk and influences on sexual decision-making for HIV prevention among students at historically black colleges and universities. *Journal of African American Studies, 9*(2), 16–28.

Tobolowsky, B. F., Outcalt, C. L., and McDonough, P. M. (2005). The role of HBCUs on the college choice process of African Americans in California. *Journal of Negro Education, 74*(21), 63–75.

Turner, S., and Bound, J. (2003). Closing the gap or widening the divide: The effects of the GI bill and World War II on the educational outcomes of black Americans. *Journal of Economic History, 63*(1), 145–177.

Turner-Musa, J. O., and Wilson, S. A. (2006). Religious orientation and social support on health-promoting behaviors of African American college students. *Journal of Community Psychology, 34*(1), 105–115.

U.S. Census Bureau. (2008). State and County Quick Facts. Retrieved July 2, 2009, from http://quickfacts.census.gov/qfd/states/28000.html.

U.S. Department of Education, National Center for Education Statistics. (1984). *Traditionally black institutions of higher education: 1860 to 1982*. Washington, DC: U.S. Government Printing Office.

U.S. Department of Education. (1996). *Biennial evaluation report, fiscal years 1995–1996*. Retrieved June 6, 2009, from http://www.ed.gov/pubs/Biennial/95-96/index.html.

U.S. Department of Education. (2008). *Education Department Budget History, FY 1980–FY 2009*. Washington, DC: U.S. Government Printing Office.

U.S. Department of Education, National Center for Education Statistics, Integrated Postsecondary Education Data System. (2009a). *Awards/degrees conferred by program, 1987–2007*. Washington, DC. Retrieved from http://nces.ed.gov/ipeds/datacenter.

U.S. Department of Education, National Center for Education Statistics, Integrated Postsecondary Education Data System. (2009b). *Current fund revenues, 2002–2007*. Washington, DC. Retrieved from http://nces.ed.gov/ipeds/datacenter.

U.S. Department of Education. (2009c). *Howard University fiscal year 2010 budget request*. Washington, DC: U.S. Government Printing Office.

U.S. Department of the Interior, Bureau of Education. (1917). *Negro education: A study of the private and higher schools for colored people in the United States*. (2 vol.). Washington, DC: U.S. Government Printing Office.

Urban, W. J. (1994). *Black scholar*. Athens: University of Georgia Press.

Valentine, P. A., Wright, D. L., and Henley, G. L. (2003). Patterns of safer sex practices among allied health students at historically black colleges and universities. *Journal of Allied Health, 32*(3), 173–178.

Wade, B. H. (2002). How does racial identity affect historically black colleges and universities' student perceptions of September 11, 2001? *Journal of Black Studies, 33*(1), 25–43.

Wagner, M., Liles, R. G., Broadnax, R. L., and Nuriddin-Little, A. (2006). Use of alcohol and other drugs: Undergraduate HBCU students. *Negro Educational Review, 57*(3/4), 229–241.

Walker, V. S. (2001). African American teaching in the South: 1940–1960. *American Educational Research Journal, 38*(4), 751–779.

Walton, A., and Gasman, M. (2008). *Philanthropy, volunteerism, and fundraising in American higher education*. New York: Pearson Publishing.

Wang, Y., Browne, D. C., Storr, C. L., and Wagner, F. A. (2005). Gender and the tobacco-depression relationship: A sample of African American college students at a historically black college or university. *Addictive Behaviors, 30*(7), 1437–1441.

Ware, L. (1994). The most visible vestige: Black colleges after *Fordice*. *Boston College Law Review, 35*(3), 633–680.

Watkins, W. (2001). *White architects of black education: Ideology and power in America*. New York: Teachers College Press.

Watson, W. H. (1999). *Against the odds: Blacks in the profession of medicine in the United States*. Piscataway, NJ: Transaction Publishers.

Watson, Y., and Gregory, S. T. (2005). *Daring to educate: The legacy of early Spelman College presidents*. Sterling, VA: Stylus Publishing.

Watt, S. K. (2006). Racial identity attitudes, womanist identity attitudes, and self-esteem in African American college women attending historically black-single sex and coeducational institutions. *Journal of College Student Development, 47*(3), 319–334.

Webster, D. S., Stockard, R. L., and Henson, J. W. (1981). Black student elite: Enrollment shifts of high achieving, high socioeconomic status black students from black to white colleges during the 1970s. *College and University, 56*(3), 283–291.

Weerts, D., and Conrad, C. F. (2002). Desegregation in Higher Education. In J.J.F. Forest and K. Kinsey (Eds.), *Higher education in the United States: An encyclopedia* (pp. 161–167). Santa Barbara: ABC-CLIO.

Wilburn, A. Y. (1974). Careers in science and engineering for black Americans. *Science, 184*(4142), 1148–1154.

Williams, J., and Ashley, D. (2004). *I'll find a way or make one: A tribute to historically black colleges and universities.* New York: HarperCollins.

Williams, L. E. (1988). Public policies and financial exigencies: Black colleges twenty years later, 1965–1985. *Journal of Black Studies, 19*(2), 135–149.

Williamson, J. A. (2004a). Brown, black, and yellow: Desegregation in a multiethnic context. *History of Education Quarterly, 44*(1), 109–112.

Williamson, J. A. (2004b). This has been quite a year for heads falling: Institutional autonomy in the civil rights era. *History of Education Quarterly 44*(4), 554–576.

Williamson, J. A. (2008). *Radicalizing the ebony tower: Black colleges and the black freedom struggle in Mississippi.* New York: Teachers College Press.

Willie, C. V. (1994). Black colleges are not just for blacks anymore. *Journal of Negro Education, 63*(2), 153–163.

Willie, C. V., and Edmonds, R. R. (1978). *Black colleges in America: Challenge, development, survival.* New York: Teachers College Press.

Willie, C. V., Reddick, R., and Brown, R. (2006). *The black college mystique.* Lanham, MD: Rowman & Littlefield.

Wilson, V. R. (2007). The effect of attending an HBCU on persistence and graduation outcomes of African American college students. *Review of Black Political Economy, 34*(1/2), 11–52.

Wolanin, T. R. (1998). The federal investment in minority-serving institutions. *New Directions for Higher Education, 26*(2), 17–32.

Woodson, C. G. (1933). *The miseducation of the Negro.* Lawrenceville, NJ: Africa World Press.

Additional Readings

AAUP Committee (Jan.–Feb., 1995). The historically black colleges and universities: A future in the balance. *Academe, 81*(1), 49–58.

Abelman, R., and Dalessandro, A. (2007). The institutional vision of historically black colleges and universities. *Journal of Black Studies, 20*(10), 1–30.

Act of Incorporation of Howard University, 20 U.S.C. 123.

Adebayo, A. O., Adekoya, A. A., and Ayadi, F. (2001). Historically black colleges and universities as agents of change for the development of minority business. *Journal of Black Studies, 32*(2), 166–183.

Akbar, R., and Sims, M. J. (2008). Surviving Katrina and keeping our eyes on the prize: The strength of legacy and tradition in New Orleans's HBCU teacher preparation programs. *Urban Education, 43*(4), 445–462.

Allen, W. R. (2005). A forward glance in a mirror: Diversity challenged—access, equity, and success in higher education. *Educational Researcher, 34*(7), 18–23.

Allen, W. R., Epps, E. G., and Haniff, N. Z. (Eds.). (1991). *College in black and white: African-American students in predominantly white and in historically black public universities.* Albany: State University of New York Press.

Allen, W. R., Jewell, J. O., Griffin, K. A., and Wolf, D. S. (2007). Historically black colleges and universities: Honoring the past, engaging the present, touching the future. *Journal of Negro Education, 76*(3), 263–280.

Anderson, E., and Moss, A. (1999). *Dangerous donations: Northern philanthropy and southern black education, 1902–1930.* Columbia: University of Missouri Press.

Anderson, J. D. (1980). Philanthropic control over private black higher education. In R. Arnove (Ed.), *Philanthropy and cultural imperialism: The foundations at home and abroad* (pp. 147–177). Boston: G. K. Hall & Co.

Armstrong, K. L. (2002). An examination of the social psychology of blacks' consumption to sport. *Journal of Sport Management, 16*(4), 267–289.

Aruguete, M. S., Debord, K. A., Yates, A., and Edman, J. (2005). Ethnic and gender differences in eating attitudes among black and white college students. *Eating Behaviors, 6*(4), 328–336.

Ayadi, F. (1994). The role of historically black colleges and universities in a renewed black capitalism. *Business and Economic Review, 8*(1), 1–19.

Azibo, D. A. (2008). Psychological Africanity (racial identity) and its influence on support for reparations. *Journal of Negro Education, 77*(2), 117–130.

Bakari, R. (2003). Preservice teachers' attitudes toward teaching African American students. *Urban Education, 38*(6), 640–555.

Bart, B. D., Philbrick, J. H., and Tapp, C. D. (1993). The impact of newsletters on community attitudes: The case of a historically black college. *Journal of Marketing for Higher Education, 4*(1/2), 339–350.

Bennett, P., and Xie, Y. (2003). Revisiting racial differences in college attendance: The role of historically black colleges and universities. *American Sociological Review, 68*(4), 567–580.

Bieze, M. (2005a). Booker T. Washington: Philanthropy and Aesthetics. In M. Gasman and K. V. Sedgwick (Eds.),*Uplifting a people: African American philanthropy and education.* New York: Peter Lang.

Bieze, M. (2005b). Ruskin in the black belt: Booker T. Washington, arts and crafts, and the new Negro. *Source: Notes in the History of Art, 24*(4), 24–34.

Bieze, M. (2006). Booker T. Washington and the Art of Self-Representation. In D. Cunningen, M. Glascoe, and D. Rutledge (Eds.), *The racial politics of Booker T. Washington.* London: Elsevier.

Bigler, M., and Jeffries, J. L. (2008). "An Amazing Specimen": NFL Draft Experts' Evaluations of black quarterbacks. *Journal of African American Studies, 12*(2), 120–141.

Billingsley, A., and Elam, J. C. (1986). *Black colleges and public policy.* Chicago: Follett Press.

Boger, C., Catrelia S. H., and Enid, B. J. (1999). A study of the relationship between alumni giving and selected characteristics of alumni donors of Livingstone College, NC. *Journal of Black Studies, 29*(4), 523–539.

Bonner, F. A., II, and Murry, J. W., Jr. (1998). Historically black colleges and universities: Is their mission unique? *National Association of Student Affairs Professionals Journal, 1*(1), 37–49.

Bougere, A. A., Rowley, L. M., and Lee, G. M. (2004). Prevalence and chronicity of dating violence among a sample of African-American university students. *Western Journal of Black Studies, 28*(4), 458–478.

Boyd, R. L. (2007). Historically black colleges and universities and the black business elite. *Sociological Perspectives, 50*(4), 545–560.

Brazzell, J. C. (1992). Bricks without straw: Missionary-sponsored black higher education in the post-emancipation era. *Journal of Higher Education, 63*(1), 26–49.

Bridges, B., Cambridge, B., Kuh, G. D., and Leegwater, L. H. (2005). Student engagement at minority-serving institutions: Emerging lessons from the BEAMS project. *New Directions for Institutional Research, 125*, 25–43.

Brower, A. M., and Ketterhagen, A. (2004). Is there an inherent mismatch between how black and white students expect to succeed in college and what their colleges expect from them? *Journal of Social Issues, 60*(1), 95–116.

Brown, J. F. (2008). Developing an English-as-a-Second-Language program for foreign-born nursing students at a historically black university in the United States. *Journal of Transcultural Nursing, 19*(2), 184–191.

Brown, L. (1998). *Long walk: The story of the presidency of Willa B. Player at Bennett College.* Greensboro, NC: Bennett College's Women's Leadership Institute.

Brown, M. C., II, and Hendrickson, R. M. (1997). Public historically black colleges at the crossroads. *Journal for Just and Caring Education, 3*(1), 95–113.

Brown, W. R. (1994). Race consciousness in higher education: Does 'sound educational policy' support the continued existence of historically black colleges? *Emory Law Journal, 43*, 1–81.

Browning, J., and Williams, J. (1978). History and goals of black institutions of higher learning. In C.V. Willie and R. Edwards (Eds.), *black colleges in America: Challenge, development, survival* (pp. 68–93). New York: Teacher's College Press.

Buchanan, L., and Hutcheson, P. (1999). Re-considering the Washington–Du Bois Debate: Two black colleges in 1910–1911. In W. Urban (Ed.), *Essays in 20th century Southern education: Exceptionalism and its limits.* New York: Garland Press.

Bullock, H. (1967). *A history of Negro education in the south: From 1619 to the present.* Cambridge, MA: Harvard University Press.

Butchart, R. (1980). *Northern schools, Southern blacks and Reconstruction: Freedmen's education, 1862–1975.* Santa Barbara: Greenwood Press.

Civil Rights Act of 1964, P.L. 88–352.

Clark, F. G. (1958). The development and present status of publicly-supported higher education for Negroes. *The Journal of Negro Education, 27*(3), 221–232.

Coaxum, J. (2001). The misalignment between the Carnegie classifications and black colleges. *Urban Education, 36*(5), 572–584.

Cohen, R. T. (2000). *The black colleges of Atlanta.* Charleston, SC: Arcadia Publishing.

Cokley, K. O. (2002). Testing Cross's Revised Racial Identity Model: An examination of the relationship between racial identity and internalized racialism. *Journal of Counseling Psychology, 49*(4), 476–484.

Constantine, M. G., and Watt, S. K. (2002). Cultural congruity, womanist identity attitudes, and life satisfaction among African American college women attending historically black and predominantly white institutions. *Journal of College Student Development, 43*(2), 184–194.

Cook, W. C. (2006). Florida's dramatic shift in student demographics: Implications for mathematics teacher education. *Journal of Instructional Psychology, 33*(2), 124–135.

Cox, M. S. (2006). "Keep our black warriors out of the draft": The Vietnam anti-war movement at Southern University, 1968–1973. *Educational Foundations, 20*(1/2), 123–144.

Coleman, M. A. (2007). Transforming to teach: Teaching religion to today's black college student. *Teaching Theology and Religion, 10*(2), 95–100.

College Cost Reduction Act, P.L. 110-84.

Conrad, C. F., and Shrode, P. E. (1990). The long road: Desegregating higher education. *Thought and Action, 6*(1), 35–45.

Curtin, M., and Gasman, M. (2003). Historically black college MBA programs: Prestige, rankings, and the meaning of success. *Journal of Education for Business, 79*(2), 79–84.

Darden, J. T., Bagakas, J. G., and Marajh, O. (1992). Historically black colleges and the dilemma of desegregation. *Equity & Excellence, 25*, 106–112.

Davis, A. L. (1985). The role of black colleges and black law schools in the training of black lawyers and judges: 1960–1980. *The Journal of Negro History, 70*(1/2), 24–34.

Davis, J. J., and Markham, P. L. (1991). Student attitudes toward foreign language study at historically and predominantly black institutions. *Foreign Language Annals, 24*(3), 227–237.

Davis, L. J., and Galloway, S. W. (1995). Prospering through partnering: A strategy for historically/predominantly black colleges and universities. *The Journal of Continuing Higher Education, 43*(2), 21–26.

Du Bois, W.E.B. (1903). The talented tenth. In *The Negro problem: A series of articles by representative American Negroes of today.* New York: J. Pott & Company, 1903, 33–75.

Du Bois, W.E.B. (1973). The future and function of the private Negro college. In H. Aptheker (Ed.), *The education of black people, ten critiques, 1906–1960.* New York: Monthly Review Press.

Duncan, L. E., and Johnson, D. (2007). Black undergraduate students' attitude toward counseling and counselor preference. *College Student Journal, 41*(3), 696–719.

Dwyer, B. (2006). Framing the effect of multiculturalism on diversity outcomes among students at historically black colleges and universities. *Educational Foundations, 20*(1/2), 37–60.

Elbert, M. M. (2005). The politics of educational decision making: Historically black colleges and universities and federal assistance programs. Westport, CT: Praeger.

Epstein, E., and Gasman, M. (2005). A not-so-systematic effort to study art: Albert Barnes and Lincoln University. *History of Higher Education Annual, 24*, 173–190.

Exec. Order No. 12,232, 3 C.F.R., (1980 comp.)

Exec. Order No. 12,320, 3 C.F.R., (1981 comp.)

Exec. Order No. 12,677, 3 C.F.R., (1989 comp.)

Exec. Order No. 12,876, 3 C.F.R., (1993 comp.)

Exec. Order No. 13,256, 3 C.F.R., (2002 comp.)

Fairclough, A. (2000). "Being in the field of education and also being a Negro . . . seems . . . tragic": Black teachers in the Jim Crow South. *The Journal of American History, 87*(1), 65–91, 26.

Fairclough, A. (2001). Tuskegee's Robert R. Moton and the travails of the early black college president. *Journal of Blacks in Higher Education, 31*, 94–105.

Fienberg, L. (1993). *United States v. Fordice* and the desegregation of public higher education: Groping for root and branch. *Boston College Law Review, 34*(4), 803–851.

Fleming, J. (2001). The impact of a historically black college on African American students: The case of Lemoyne-Owen College. *Urban Education, 36*(5), 597–610.

Flowers, L. A., Jackson, J.F.L., and Bridges, B. K. (2002). Influences on precollege students' use of study strategies. *Journal of Critical Inquiry into Curriculum and Instruction, 4*(1), 10–15.

Franklin, V. P. (2003). Patterns of student activism at historically black universities in the United States and South Africa, 1960–1977. *Journal of African American History, 88*(2), 204–217.

Freeman, K., and Cohen, R. T. (2001). Bridging the gap between economic development and cultural empowerment: HBCUs challenges for the future. *Urban Education*, 36(5), 585–596.

Gabbidon, S. L., Penn, E. B., and Richards, W. A. (2003). Career choices and characteristics of African-American undergraduates majoring in criminal justice at historically black colleges and universities. *Journal of Criminal Justice Education, 14*(2), 229–244.

Garibaldi, A. (1984). *Black colleges and universities: Challenges for the future.* New York: Praeger.

Gasman, M. (2002a). A word for every occasion: Appeals by John D. Rockefeller, Jr. to white donors on behalf of the United Negro College Fund. *History of Higher Education Annual, 22*, 67–90.

Gasman, M. (2002b). An untapped resource: Bringing African Americans into the college and university giving process. *The CASE International Journal of Educational Advancement, 2*(3), 280–292.

Gasman, M. (2002c). W.E.B. Du Bois and Charles S. Johnson: Opposing views on philanthropic support for black higher education. *History of Education Quarterly, 42*(4), 493–516.

Gasman, M. (2005a). Coffee table to classroom: A review of recent scholarship on historically black colleges and universities. *Educational Researcher, 34*(7), 32–39.

Gasman, M. (2005b). Historically black colleges and universities: A bibliography. *Review of Black Political Economy, 34*(1/2), 111–147.

Gasman, M. (2005c). The role of faculty in fundraising at black colleges: What is it and what can it become? *International Journal of Educational Advancement*, 5(2), 171–179.

Gasman, M. (2006a). Education in black and white: New perspectives on the history of historically black colleges and universities. *Teachers College Record*, January.

Gasman, M. (March–April, 2006b). Salvaging 'academic disaster areas': The black college response to Christopher Jencks' and David Riesman's 1967 *Harvard Educational Review* article. *Journal of Higher Education, 77*(1), 317–352.

Gasman, M. (2006c). Truth, generalizations, and stigmas: An analysis of the media's coverage of Morris Brown College and black colleges overall. *Review of the Black Political Economy, 34*(1–2), 111–147.

Gasman, M., and Drezner, N. D. (2007a). Hurricane Katrina and our nation's black colleges. In R. Swan and K. Bates (Eds.), *Social justice and hurricane Katrina* (pp. 337–344). Durham, NC: Carolina Academic Press.

Gasman, M., and Drezner, N. D. (2007b). A rising tide: New Orleans' black colleges and their efforts to rebuild after hurricane Katrina. *Multicultural Review, 16*(1), 34–39.

Gasman, M., and Epstein, E. (2002). Modern art in the old south: The role of the arts in Fisk University's campus curriculum. *Educational Researcher, 31*(2), 13–20.

Gasman, M., and Epstein, E. (2004). Creating an image for black colleges: A visual examination of the United Negro College Fund's publicity, 1944–1960. *Educational Foundations, 18*(2), 41–61.

Gasman, M., and Jennings, M. E. (2006). New research, new questions: Social foundations scholarship on historically black colleges and universities (HBCUs). *Educational Foundations, 20*(1/2), 3–8.

Gasman, M., and McMickens, T. (forthcoming). Liberal or professional education? The missions of public black colleges and universities and their impact on the future of African Americans. *SOULS: A Critical Journal of Black Politics, Culture, and Society.*

Gasman, M., and Tudico, C. (2008). *Historically black colleges and universities: Triumphs, troubles, and taboos.* New York: Palgrave.

Gerlich, R. N., Turner, N., and Gopalan, S. (2007). Ethics and music: A comparison of students at predominately white and black colleges, and their attitudes toward file sharing. *Academy of Educational Leadership Journal, 11*(2), 1–11.

Giddings, P. *In search of sisterhood: Delta Sigma Theta and the challenge of the black sorority movement.* New York: HarperCollins.

Gilbert, S. C., So, D., Russell, T. M., and Wessel, T. R. (2006). Racial identity and psychological symptoms among African Americans attending a historically black university. *Journal of College Counseling, 9*(2), 111–122.

Giles, M. S. (2006). Howard Thurman: The making of a Morehouse man, 1919–1923. *Educational Foundations, 20*(1/2), 105–122.

Gipson, G. W., Reese, S., Vieweg, V.W.R., Anum, E. A., Pandurangi, A. K., Olbrisch, M. E., Sood, B., and Silverman, J. J. (2005). Body image and attitude toward obesity in an historically black university. *Journal of the National Medical Association, 97*(2), 225–236.

Goodwin, R. K. (1991). Roots and wings. *Journal of Negro Education, 60*(2), 126–132.

Greer, T. M. (2008). Racial and ethnic-related stressors as predictors of perceived stress and academic performance for African American students at a historically black college and university. *Journal of Negro Education, 77*(1), 60–71.

Gregory, S., and Watson, Y. (2005). *Daring to educate: The legacy of the early Spelman College presidents.* Sterling, VA: Stylus Publishing.

Gurin, P. (1966). Social class constraints on the occupational aspirations of students attending some predominantly Negro colleges. *The Journal of Negro Education, 35*(4), 336–350.

Gurin, P., and Epps, E. (1966). Some characteristics of students from poverty backgrounds attending predominantly Negro colleges in the Deep South. *Social Forces, 45*(1), 27–40.

Hall, B. (2005). When the majority is the minority: White graduate students' social adjustment at a historically black university. *Journal of College Student Development, 46*(1), 28–42.

Harper, S., and Gasman, M. (2009). Consequences of conservatism: Black male undergraduates and the politics of historically black colleges and universities. *Journal of Negro Education, 77*(2), 336–351.

Harper, S. R. (2001). On analyzing HBCU admissions and recruitment material. *National Association of Student Affairs Professionals, 4*(1), 55–64.

Harrington, E., and DiBona, J. (1993). Bringing multiculturalism to the historically black university in the United States. *Educational Horizons, 71*(3), 150–156.

Harris, R. P., and Worthen, H. D. (2004). Working through the challenges: Struggle and resilience within the historically black land grant institutions. *Education, 124*(3), 447–455.

Hendricks, D. L., and Hendricks, C. S. (2005). The relationship of hope and self-efficacy to health promoting behaviors among student-athletes attending historically black colleges and universities. *Journal of Multicultural Nursing and Health, 11*(3), 23–34.

Hendrix, W. F., and Javier, W. (1986). Recruitment: A significant and overlooked component of black college survival. *The Western Journal of Black Studies, 10*(2), 55–58.

Herndon, M. K., and Hirt, J. B. (2004). Black students and their families. *Journal of Black Studies, 34*(4), 489–513.

Higher Education Act of 1965, P.L. 89-329, P.L. 105-244.

Hirt, J. B., Amelink, C. T., McFeeters, B. B., and Strayhorn, T. L. (2008). A system of other mothering: Student affairs administrators' perceptions of relationships with students at historically black colleges. *National Association for Student Affairs Professionals Journal, 45*(2), 210–236.

Hirt, J. B., Bennett, B. R., Amelink, C. T., and Strayhorn, T. L. (2006). What really matters? The nature of rewards for student affairs administrators at historically black colleges and universities. *National Association of Student Affairs Professionals Journal, 9,* 83–99.

Hirt, J. B., Strayhorn, T. L., Amelink, C. T., and Bennett, B. R. (2006). The nature of student affairs work at historically black colleges and universities. *Journal of College Student Development, 47*(6), 661–676.

Homan, L. M., and Reilly, T. (2001). *Black knights: The story of the Tuskegee Airmen.* New York: Pelican Publishing Company.

Hossler, D. (1997). Historically black public colleges and universities: Scholarly inquiry and personal reflections. *Journal for Just and Caring Education, 3*(1), 114–126.

Hudgins, J. L. (1994). The segmentation of southern sociology? Social research at historically black colleges and universities. *Social Forces, 72*(3), 885–893.

Hughes, L. (August, 1934). Cowards from the colleges. *Crisis, 8,* 227.

Hutcheson, P. (2008). Shall I Compare Thee?: Reflections on Naming and Power. In M. Gasman, B. Baez, and C. S. Turner (Eds.), *Understanding minority serving institutions* (pp. 54–70). Albany: State University of New York Press.

Hytche, W. P. (1990). Historically black institutions forge linkages with African nations. *Educational Record, 71*(2), 19–21.

Injay (Ed.). (1999). *Black colleges and universities: Charcoals to diamonds.* Huntsville, AL: SSSH! Enterprises.

Jarmon, C. (2003). Sociology at Howard University: From E. Franklin Frazier and beyond. *Teaching Sociology, 31*(4), 366–374.

Jencks, C., and Riesman, D. (1968). *The academic revolution.* Chicago: University of Chicago Press.

Jenkins, M. D. (1954). Enrollment in institutions of higher education of Negroes, 1953–54. *Journal of Negro Education, 23*(2), 139–151.

Johnson, A. M., Jr. (1993). Bid whist, tonk, and the *United States v. Fordice*: Why integrationism fails African-Americans again. *California Law Review, 81*(6), 1401–1470.

Johnson, C. (2002) *African Americans and ROTC: Military, Naval, and Aeroscience programs at historically black colleges, 1916–1973.* Jefferson, NC: McFarland and Company, Inc.

Johnson, C. S. (1969). *The Negro college graduate.* New York: Negro Universities Press.

Johnson, G. S., and Rainey, S. A. (2007). Hurricane Katrina impact on three historically black colleges and universities (HBCUs): Voices from displaced students. *Race, Gender & Class, 14*(1/2), 100–119.

Jones, B. W. (1998). Rediscovering our heritage: Community service and the historically black university. In E. Zlotkowski (Ed.), *Successful service-learning programs: New models of excellence in higher education* (pp. 109–124). Bolton, MA: Anker Publishing Company, Inc.

Jones, J. H. (1992). *Bad blood: The Tuskegee syphilis experiment.* New York: Simon & Schuster.

Jones, M. (1971). The responsibility of the black college to the black community: Then and now. *Daedalus, 100,* 732–744.

Jones, T. J. (1969). *Negro education: A study of the private and public higher education schools for colored people in the United States.* New York: Arno Press.

Jones-Wilson, F. C. (1984). The nature and importance of the foundations of education in a teacher education program at a black university. *Teacher Education Quarterly, 11*(2), 41–45.

Kennard, T. H. (1995). *The handbook of historically black colleges and universities: Comprehensive profiles and photos of black colleges and universities.* Wilmington, DE: Jireh & Associates, Inc.

Kenya, S., Bordsky, M., Divale, W., Allegrante, J. P., and Fullilove, R. E. (2003). Effects of immigration on selected health risk behaviors of black college students. *Journal of American College Health, 52*(3), 113–120.

Klein, A. (1969). *Survey of Negro colleges and universities.* New York: Negro Universities Press.

Knox, P. L., Fagley, N. S., and Miller, P. M. (2004). Care and justice moral orientation among African American college students. *Journal of Adult Development, 11*(1), 41–45.

Kranz, P. L., Lund, N. L., and Johnson, B. O. (1996). Enhancing racial understanding: A class visit to a black university. *The Journal of Experiential Education, 19*(3), 152–157.

Langima, K., and Durham, E. (2007). Bridging the gap: African and African American communication in historically black colleges and universities. *Journal of Black Studies, 37*(6), 805–826.

Larid, T. G., and Shelton, A. J. (2006). From an Adlerian perspective: Birth order, dependency, and binge drinking on a historically black university campus. *Journal of Individual Psychology, 62*(10), 18–35.

Lash, J. S. (1951). The umpteenth crisis in Negro higher education. *Journal of Negro Education, 22*(8), 432–436, 458.

Lefever, H. G. (2005). *Undaunted by the fight: Spelman College and the Civil Rights Movement, 1957–1957.* Mercer, GA: Mercer University Press.

Lesane-Brown, C. L., Brown, T. N., Caldwell, C. H., and Sellars, R. M. (2005). The comprehensive race socialization inventory. *Journal of Black Studies, 36*(2), 163–190.

Levering, L. (1994). *W.E.B. Du Bois. Biography of a race, 1868–1919.* New York: Henry Holt.

Lincoln, C. E., and Lawrence, H. M. (1990). *The black church in the African American experience*. Durham, NC: Duke University Press.

Lindsey, D. F. (1995). *Indians at Hampton Institute, 1877–1923*. Urbana-Champaign: University of Illinois Press.

Little, M. H. (2002). The extra-curricular activities of black college students, 1868–1940. *Journal of African American history, 87*, 43–56.

Logan, R. (2005). *Howard University: The first hundred years, 1867–1967*. New York: New York University Press.

Lowe, J. S. (2008). A participatory planning approach to enhancing a historically black university-community partnership: The case of the e-City Initiative. *Planning Practice & Research, 23*(4), 549–558.

Luti, A. N. (1999). When a door closes, a window opens: Do today's private historically black colleges and universities run afoul of conventional equal protection analysis? *Howard Law Journal, 42*, 469.

McAlexander, J. H., Koenig, H. F., and Schouten, J. W. (2006). Black college alumni giving: A study of the perceptions, attitudes, and giving behaviors of alumni donors at selected historically black colleges and universities. *International Journal of Educational Advancement, 6*(3), 200–220.

McKenzie, T. L. (1993). *United States v. Fordice:* Does the end of "separate and unequal" in higher education also spell the end of historically black colleges? *Western State University Law Review, 20*, 735–747.

McPherson, J. M. (1970). White liberals and black power in Negro education, 1865–1915. *The American Historical Review, 75*(5), 1357–1386.

Medford, G. S. (1998). A view of curricula in educational theatre from seven historically black colleges and universities, 1900–1990. *The Negro Educational Review, 49*(3–4), 139–146.

Miller, P. B. (1995). To "bring the race along rapidly": Sport, student culture, and educational mission at historically black colleges during the interwar years. *History of Education Quarterly, 35*(2), 111–133.

Minor, J. T. (2004). Dilemmas of decision-making in historically black colleges and universities: Defining the context. *Journal of Negro Education, 73*(1), 40–52.

Moore, J. A. (2000). Are state-supported historically black colleges and universities justifiable after *Fordice*? A higher education dilemma. *Florida State University Law Review, 27*, 547–567.

Morrill Act of 1862, 7 U.S.C. 301 *et seq.*

Morrill Act of 1890, 7 U.S.C. 322 *et seq.*

Mullen, B. V. (2007). Black list Redux: W.E.B. Du Bois and the price of academic freedom. *Social Text, 25*(1), 85–103.

Murphy, A. J. (2005). Money, money, money: An exploratory study on the financial literacy of black college students. *College Student Journal, 39*(3), 478–488.

Mykerezi, E., and Mills, B. F. (2008). The wage earnings impact of historically black colleges and universities. *Southern Economic Journal, 75*(1), 173–187.

Mykerezi, E., and Mills, B. F. (2004). Education and economic well-being in racially diverse rural counties: The role of historically black colleges and universities. *Review of Regional Studies, 34*(3), 303–319.

Negga, F., Applewhite, S., and Livingston, I. (2007). African American college students and stress: School racial composition, self-esteem and social support. *College Student Journal, 41*(4), 823–830.

Nettles, M. T., Perna, L. W., and Freeman, K. E. (1999). *Two decades of progress: African-Americans moving forward in higher education.* Fairfax, VA: College Fund/UNCF.

Nnazor, R., Sloan, J., and Higgins, P. (2004). Historically black colleges and universities and the challenge of teacher licensure tests. *Western Journal of Black Studies, 28*(4), 449–452.

Olswang, S., and Taylor, E. (1999). Peril or promise: The effect of desegregation litigation on historically black colleges. *The Western Journal of Black Studies, 23*(2), 73–82.

Patterson, C. M. (1994). Desegregation as a two-way street: The aftermath of *United States v. Fordice. Cleveland State Law Review, 42*(3), 377–433.

Patterson, F. D. (1952). The private Negro college in a racially-integrated system of higher education. *Journal of Negro Education, 21*(3), 363–369.

Patterson, F. D. (1958). Colleges for Negro youth and the future. *Journal of Negro Education, 27*(2), 107–114.

Patterson, F. D. (1959). Foundation policies in regard to Negro institutions of higher learning. *Journal of Educational Sociology, 32*(6), 290–296.

Payne, N. J. (1987). The role of black colleges in an expanding economy. *Educational Record, 68*(4), 104–106.

Pearson, R. L. (1983). Reflections on black colleges. The historical perspective of Charles S. Johnson. *History of Education Quarterly, 23*(1), 55–68.

Peeps, J.M.S. (1981). Northern philanthropy and the emergence of Black higher education: Do gooder's, compromisers, or co-conspirators? *Journal of Negro Education, 50*(3), 251–269.

Penn, E. B., and Gabbidon, S. L. (2007). Criminal justice education at historically black colleges and universities: Three decades of progress. *Journal of Criminal Justice Education, 18*(1), 137–162.

Peters, A. W. (2005). Teaching biochemistry at a minority-serving institution: An evaluation of the role of collaborative learning as a tool for science. *Journal of Chemical Education, 82*(4), 571–574.

Pike, G. D. (1973). *Jubilee singers, and their campaign for twenty thousand dollars.* London: Hodder and Stoughton.

Powe, B. D., Louis, R., and Cooper, D. L. (2007). Attitudes and beliefs about smoking among African-American college students at historically black colleges and universities. *Journal of the National Medical Association, 99*(4), 338–344.

Powell, R. J., and Reynolds, J. (1999). *To conserve a legacy: American art from historically black colleges and universities.* Cambridge: Massachusetts Institute of Technology.

Preer, J. (1990). "Just and equitable division": Jim Crow and the 1890 Land-Grant College Act. *Prologue, 22*(4), 323–337.

Preer, J. L. (1982). *Lawyers v. educators: Black colleges and desegregation in public higher educa-tion.* Westport, CT: Greenwood.

President's Board of Advisors on Historically Black Colleges and Universities. *The Mission Continues: Annual Report to the President on the results of participation of historically black colleges and universities in federal programs 2002–03.* Washington, DC, 2005.

Price, G. N. (1998). Black colleges and universities: The road to Philistia? *Negro Educational Review, 49,* 9–21.

Price, G. N. (2000). The idea of the historically black university. *Negro Educational Review, 51*(3), 99–113.

Redd, K. E. (1998). Historically black colleges and universities: Making a comeback. *New Directions for Higher Education, 102,* 33–43.

Reid, L. V., Hatch, J., and Parrish, T. (2003). The role of a historically black university and black church in community-based health initiatives: The Project DIRECT Experience. *Journal of Public Health Management and Practice, 9,* S70–S73.

Reverby, S. M. (2000). *Tuskegee's truths: Rethinking the Tuskegee syphilis study.* Chapel Hill: The University of North Carolina Press.

Richardson, J. M. (1980). *A history of Fisk University, 1865–1946.* Birmingham, AL: The University of Alabama Press.

Richmond, K. A. (1998). Charting a new millennium agenda for historically black colleges and universities. *The Negro Educational Review, 49*(3), 147–152.

Roebuck, J. B., and Murty, K. S. (1993). *Historically black colleges and universities: Their place in American higher education.* Westport, CT: Praeger.

Rosenthal, J. (1975). Southern black student activism: Assimilation vs. nationalism. *Journal of Negro Education, 44*(2), 113–129.

Ross, M. (2003). *Success factors of young African American women at a historically black college.* Westport: CT: Praeger.

Rucker, M. L., and Gendrin, D. M. (2003). The impact of ethnic identification on student learning in the HBCU classroom. *Journal of Instructional Psychology, 30*(3), 207–215.

Sagini, M. M. (1996). *African and the African American university: A historical and sociologi-cal analysis.* New York: University Press of America.

Samuels, A. L. (2004). *Is separate unequal? Black colleges and the challenge to desegregation.* Lawrence: The University Press of Kansas.

Sanders, C. D., and Green, B. E. (2008). From "Block the Vote" to "Protect the Vote": Histor-ically black student voting suppression and disenfranchisement in Texas. *Harvard Journal of African American Public Policy, 14,* 51–59.

Saunders, K. P., and Westbrook, T. S. (2001). Historically black colleges and universities: Lessons from the past, hope for the future. *ISPA Journal, 13*(1), 2–19.

Sav, T. (2000). Tests of fiscal discrimination in higher education finance: Funding historically black colleges and universities. *Journal of Education Finance, 26,* 157–172.

Schuh, J. H. (2003). Funding provided by historically black colleges and universities for stu-dent affairs: A comparison with counterpart historically white colleges and universities. *National Association of Student Affairs Professionals Journal, 6*(1), 25–33.

Schwartz, R. A., and Washington, C. M. (1999). African-American freshmen in a historically black college. *Journal of the First-Year Experience and Students in Transition, 11*(1), 39–62.

Sekora, J. (1968). On Negro colleges: A reply to Jencks and Riesman. *Antioch Review, 28*, 1.

Shaw, R. G. (1991). Forging new alliances with historically black colleges. *Community, Technical, and Junior College Journal, 61*(6), 41–43.

Simmons, C., Worrell, F. C., and Berry, J. M. (2008). Psychometric properties of scores on three black racial identity scales. *Assessment, 15*(3), 259–276.

Simmons, H. L. (1984). The accreditation process as a factor in the improvement of traditionally black institutions. *Journal of Negro Education, 53*(4), 400–405.

Sims, S. J. (1994). *Diversifying historically black colleges and universities: A new higher education paradigm.* Westport, CT: Greenwood Press.

Sissoko, M. (2005). Minority enrollment demand for higher education at historically black colleges and universities from 1976 to 1998: An empirical analysis. *Journal of Higher Education, 76*(2), 181–208.

Snipes, V. T., Ellis, W., and Thomas, J. (2006). Are HBCUs up to speed technologically? *Journal of Black Studies, 36*(3), 382–395.

Smith, T. A. (1993). *United States* v. *Fordice*: The interpretation of desegregation in higher education and the struggle for the survival of the historically black colleges in America. *Southern University Law Review, 20*(2), 407–439.

Snowden, M. T., Jackson, J.F.L., and Flowers, L. A. (2002). An examination of the efficiency of the proposed remedies and settlement for Ayers: Based on a study of black college students in Mississippi. *NASAP Journal, 5*(1), 7–20.

So, D.W., Gilbert, S., and Romero, S. (2005). Help-seeking attitudes among African American college students. *College Student Journal, 39*(4), 806–816.

Sorrells, A. M., Schaller, J., and Yang, N. K. (2004). Teacher efficacy ratings by African American and European American preservice teachers at a historically black university. *Urban Education, 39*(5), 509–536.

Sowell, T. W. (1973). *Black education: Myths and tragedies.* New York: David McKay Company.

Sowell, T. W. (October 3, 2003). On racial censorship and Rush Limbaugh. *Jewish World Review.* http://www.jewishworldreview.com/cols/sowell1.asp.

Stahl, J. M. (2005). Research for everyone: Perspectives from teaching at historically black colleges and universities. *Journal of Social & Clinical Psychology, 24*(1), 85–96.

Stewart, T. J., Prinzinger, J. M., Dias, J. K., Bowden, J. T., Salley, J. K., and Smith, A. E. (1989). The economic impact of a historically black college upon its local community. *Journal of Negro Education, 58*(2), 232–242.

Stuckert, R. (1964). The Negro college—A pawn of white domination. *The Wisconsin Sociologist.*

Sum, P. E., Light, S. A., and King, R. E. (2004). Race, reform, and desegregation in Mississippi higher education: Historically black institutions after *United States v. Fordice. Law & Social Inquiry, 29*(2), 403–435.

Sutton, A. M. (2005). Bridging the gap in early library education history for African Americans: The Negro teacher-librarian training program (1936–1939). *Journal of Negro Education, 74*(2), 138–150.

Swinton, O. (2007). Grading for effort: The success equals effort policy at Benedict College. *Review of the Black Political Economy, 34*(1/2), 149–164.

Taylor, E., and Olswang, S. (1999). Peril or promise: The effect of desegregation litigation on historically black colleges. *The Western Journal of Black Studies, 23*(2), 73–82.

Taylor, H. (2007). Black spaces: Examining the writing major at an urban HBCU. *Composition Studies, 35*(1), 99–112.

Thompson, D. C. (1986). *A black elite: A profile of graduate of UNCF colleges.* Westport, CT: Greenwood.

Thurgood, M. F., and Geiger, S. M. (2007). *Understanding gender at public historically black colleges and universities.* Washington, DC: Thurgood Marshall Fund.

Tindall, N.T.J. (2007). Fund-raising models at public historically black colleges and universities. *Public Relations Review, 33,* 201–205.

Trent, W. J., and Hill, J. (1994). The contributions of historically black college and universities to the production of African American scientists and engineers. In W. Pearson, Jr., and A. Fechter (Eds.), *Who Will Do Science?: Educating the Next Generation.* Baltimore University Press: Johns Hopkins.

Trent, W. J. Jr., (1955). Cooperative fund raising for higher education. *Journal of Negro Education, 24*(1), 6–15.

Trent, W. J., Jr., and Patterson, F. D. (1958). Financial support of the private Negro college. *Journal of Negro Education, 27*(3), 398–405.

Tucker, S. K. (2002). The early years of the United Negro College Fund. *The Journal of African American History, 87*(4), 416–432.

U.S. Department of Education (n.d.). *Education Department Budget History Table: FY 1980–Present.* http://www.ed.gov/about/overview/budget/history/edhistory.xls.

U.S. Department of Education. (2007). *White House initiative on historically black colleges and universities, fulfilling the covenant—The way forward: 2004–05 annual report to the president on the results of participation of historically black colleges and universities in federal programs.* ed.gov/about/inits/list/whhbcu/pba-hbcu-report-2004-05.doc.

Urban, W. J. (1989). Philanthropy and the black scholar: The case of Horace Mann Bond. *Journal of Negro Education, 58*(4), 478–493.

Verharen, C. C. (1993). A core curriculum at historically black colleges and universities: An immodest proposal. *Journal of Negro Education, 62*(2), 190–203.

Walker, T. A., Howard, D. L., Washington, C. R., and Godley, P. A. (2007). Development of a health sciences library at a historically black college and university (HBCU): Laying the foundation for increased minority health and health disparities research. *Journal of the Medical Library Association, 95*(4), 439–441.

Wallenstein, P. (2004). To sit or not to sit: The supreme court of the United States and the civil rights movement in the upper south. *Journal of Supreme Court History, 29*(2), 145–162.

Ward, A. (2000). *Dark midnight when I rise: The story of the Jubilee Singers, who introduced the world to the music of black America*. New York: Farrar, Straus, and Giroux.

Watkins, W. (1990). Teaching and learning in the black colleges: A 130-year retrospective. *Teaching Education, 3*(1), 10–25.

Watson, L. W., and Kuh, G. D. (1996). The influence of dominant race environments on student involvement, perceptions, and educational gains: A look at historically black and predominantly white liberal arts institutions. *Journal of College Student Development, 3*(4), 415–424.

Weaver, R. C. (1960). The Negro private and church-related college. A critical summary. *Journal of Negro Education, 29*(3), 394–400.

Wenglinsky, H. (1999). *Historically black colleges and universities: Their aspirations and accomplishments*. Princeton, NJ: Educational Testing Service.

Wenglinsky, H. H. (1996). The educational justification of historically black colleges and universities: A policy response to the U.S. Supreme Court. *Educational Evaluation and Policy Analysis, 18*(1), 91–103.

Williams, J. (1992). *Factors related to fund-raising outcomes at United Negro College Fund member institutions (black colleges)*. Ph.D. Dissertation, University of Maryland, College Park.

Williams, J. E., and MacLean, V. M. (2005). Studying ourselves: Sociology discipline-building in the United States. *American Sociologist, 36*(1), 111–133.

Willie, C. V. (1981). *The ivory and ebony towers*. Lexington, MA: Lexington Books.

Wilson, R. (1990). Can black colleges solve the problem of access for black students? *American Journal of Education, 98*(4), 443–457.

Wingard, E. (1982). Experience of historically black colleges in serving diversely prepared students. *New Directions for Experiential Learning, 17*, 29–36.

Wolters, R. (1975). *The new Negro on campus: Black college rebellions of the 1920s*. Princeton, NJ: Princeton University.

Wright, S. R. (2008). Self-determination, politics, and gender on Georgia's black college campuses, 1875–1900. *Georgia Historical Quarterly, 92*(1), 93–119.

Name Index

A

Adams, F., 22
Adams, W., 32
Agesa, J., 52, 53
Allen, W. R., 27, 29, 32, 33, 34, 38, 40
Alston, J. R., 24
Anderson, J. D., 6, 7, 8, 47, 73, 74, 75
Anderson-Thompkins, S., 56, 57, 58, 59
Antonio, A. L., 24, 27, 28, 30
Armstrong, S. C., 7
Ashley, D., 32, 60
Astin, H., 30, 49
Ayers, J., 18

B

Baez, B., 7, 8
Baldwin, J., 6
Baxter, F. V., 13, 15, 23
Benjamin, L., 43
Berger, J. B., 27, 38
Bertrand, R. D., 32, 71
Betsey, C., 52, 53
Billingsley, A., 49
Blake, A. C., 39
Boatsman, K., 38
Bonner, F. B., 32, 33, 34, 35, 37, 53
Bonous-Hammarth, M., 38
Boone, P. R., 27, 38
Borgstedt, K. W., 48
Bound, J., 64
Bowles, E., 32
Brady, K., 15, 24, 40

Braxton, J. M., 27, 29, 30, 31, 39
Brazziel, W. F., 76
Bridges, B. K., 33, 34
Brier, E. M., 27, 29, 30, 31, 39
Broadnax, R. L., 28
Brooks, F. E., 17, 18
Brown, I. C., 76
Brown, M. C., II, 11, 12, 13, 25, 32, 43, 45, 71, 74, 75
Brown, R., 32
Brown, T. L., 38
Browne, D. C., 34
Bush, G. W., 68
Bush, G.H.W., 68
Butler, J. S., 27
Byrd, A., 58

C

Carini, R. M., 33, 34
Carlon, A., 28
Carnegie, A., 6
Carter, D. G., 76
Carter, J., 9, 67, 68
Carter, L., 43
Chargois, J. A., 27
Chavous, T. M., 35
Christy, R. D., 63, 70
Chung, C., 28
Clinton, B., 68
Closson, R. B., 28, 39
Cokley, K. O., 27, 34
Cole, J. B., 49, 50, 51, 84

Cole, W. M., 75
Cole, B., 69
Conrad, C. F., 20, 21, 27, 29, 30, 31, 39, 40
Constantine, J. M., 27, 39
Cooper, J. E., 48
Craig, L. A., 70, 76, 81
Cross, P. H., 30

D

Daniel, R. P., 75, 76
Daniel, W. G., 75, 76
Davis, L., 43
DeCosta, F., 32
DeSousa, D. J., 38, 40
Dey, E. L., 51
Doermann, H., 25
Donahoo, S., 32, 71
Dreher, G. F., 27
Drewry, H. N., 25
Drezner, N., 56, 58
Du Bois, W.E.B., 7, 74, 75

E

Eatman, T., 15, 24
Eckes, S., 51
Edelin, K. C., 34
Edgecomb, G. S., 48
Edmonds, R. R., 32, 44, 45
Ehrenberg, R. G., 32, 39
Elkhanialy, H., 79
Eng, E., 35
Engs, R., 43
Epps, E., 29, 32

F

Fairclough, A., 73, 75
Fairfax, J. E., 58
Farazzo, D. E., 38
Ferguson, Y. O., 35
Figgures, C., 76
Fleming, J., 29, 32, 33, 36, 38
Flexner, A., 79, 80
Flores, A., 28
Flowers, L. A., 27, 38
Foster, L., 47, 48

Frazier, E. F., 44
Freeman, K., 24, 27, 29, 30, 32, 71, 74, 75
Freeman, M. L., 71
Fries-Britt, S. L., 38
Fryer, R. G., 39

G

Gabbidon, S. L., 28
Gallagher, K. S., 30
Garrett, R. U., 28
Gasman, M., 6, 7, 8, 9, 14, 24, 34, 35, 36,
  37, 43, 47, 48, 53, 55, 56, 57, 58, 59,
  60, 83, 84
Geier, S., 15, 16
Geiger, S. M., 32, 34, 37
Gibbs, W. T., 81
Gilpin, P. J., 43
Goodson, M. G., 43
Graham, A., 48
Granger, M., 52, 53
Grant, L., 52
Grayson, L. P., 81
Green, P., 65
Greenston, M., 39
Gregory, S. TT., 43
Gurin, P., 29, 32
Guy-Sheftall, B., 49, 50
Guyden, J. A., 47, 48

H

Hale, F. W., Jr., 41
Hall, B., 28
Hall-Russell, C., 58
Haniff, N. Z., 32, 34, 38
Harlan, L. R., 74
Harley, D. A., 23, 24
Harper, S. R., 33, 34, 35, 36
Harrell, J. P., 27, 38, 40
Harris, J. J., III, 24, 61, 76
Harvey, W. B., 27, 32, 52, 53
Hayek, J. C., 33, 34
Henley, G. L., 28
Henry, W. J., 39
Henson, J. W., 40
Herndon, M. K., 35, 36

Hill, S. T., 31, 37
Holliday, R. C., 28
Holloman, D., 57
Hope, J., 44
Hossler, D., 30
Huang, C. J., 28
Humphries, F. S., 62, 63, 70, 76

J

Jackson, C. L., 51, 71, 73
Jaffe, A. J., 32
Jencks, C., 44
Jenkins, M. D., 13, 23, 24, 25, 70, 78
Jewell, J. O., 32, 48
Johnson, B. J., 52, 53
Johnson, L. B., 65

K

Kasberg, R. H., 58
Kathuria, S., 52
Killenbeck, A., 41
Kim, M. M., 27, 32, 38, 40
Kimbrough, W., 32, 35, 36, 38, 39, 50, 51
Knight, J. F., 17
Kuh, G. D., 38, 40
Kujovich, G., 70

L

Ladson, G. M., 28
Lang, M., 40
Laws, M. A., 28
Lieberman, R. C., 62
Liles, R. G., 28
Lin, J., 28
Lincoln, C. E., 58
Logan, R., 69
Lott, J. L., II, 27

M

McDonough, P. M., 24, 27, 28, 29, 30, 31
McGrath, E. J., 75, 76, 77, 78, 81
McKinney, R., 43
McNeal, C., 35, 36
McNeal, G. J., 53
McPartland, J., 24

McWherter (Gov.), 16
Magrane, D., 28
Manley, A., 43
Massey, D., 48
Mays, B., 43
Mbajekwe, C. O., 45
Meier, A., 48
Mercer, C., 66
Meyers, S. G., 32
Milem, J. F., 27, 38, 49
Miller, A. L., 47, 48
Millett, C., 41
Minor, J. T., 49, 51, 69, 70, 71
Molock, S. D., 32, 39
Moton, R. R., 44
Mumper, M., 71
Myrdal, G., 44

N

Nasim, A., 27, 38, 40
Nettles, M. T., 32, 34, 37, 40, 41
Nichols, J. C., 43
Nixon, H. L., 39
Nunn, E. F., 71, 73
Nuriddin-Little, A., 28

O

Obama, B., 1, 2
Onkst, D. H., 63, 64
Outcalt, C. L., 24, 27, 29, 31, 32, 38

P

Palmer, R., 35, 36
Parker, L., 15, 24
Parker, M. H., 62
Parks, G. S., 38
Patterson, F. D., 8
Payne, N. J., 60
Peabody, J. F., 6
Perna, L., 21, 27, 29, 32, 33, 34, 37, 40, 48, 52, 80, 82
Peters, R. J., Jr., 34
Phillips, C. M., 38
Phillips, I. P., 49
Pressley, C., 58

Price, G. N., 52, 53
Provasnik, S., 28, 32, 34, 37, 47, 48, 52

Q

Quinn, S. C., 35

R

Reagan, R., 68
Reddick, R., 32
Reid, R. D., 75
Reitzes, D. C., 79
Renzulli, L. A., 52
Ricard, R. B., 45
Richardson, J. W., 24, 61
Riesman, D., 44
Riggins, R. K., 35, 36
Robbins, R., 43
Roberts, A., 27, 38, 40
Robertson, N., 34
Robinson, A., 49
Rockefeller, J. D., Jr., 6
Rockefeller, J. D., Sr., 6
Rosenwald, J., 6
Ross, L., 38
Ross, M. J., 35, 36
Rothstein, D. S., 32, 39

S

Sandelowski, M., 35
Sanders, R., 15
Savitt, T. L., 79, 80
Sedgwick, K., 60
Shafer, L. L., 28, 32, 34, 37, 47, 48, 52
Sibulkin, A., 27
Singh, K., 49
Skewes-Cox, T. E., 32, 38
Smith, G., 43
Smith, S. L., 48
Snowden, M., 51
Snyder, T. D., 28, 32, 34, 37, 47, 48, 52
Solorzano, D. G., 33, 48, 52
Stevens, A., 38
Stier, W., 53
Stockard, R. L., 40

Storr, C. L., 34
Strayhorn, T. L., 27, 35, 39, 40

T

Tabbye, C., 34
Tatum, B., 50
Tennessee, W., 24
Thelin, J. R., 62
Thomas, G. E., 24, 27, 30
Thompson, C. J., 51
Thompson, D. C., 6, 44
Thompson-Robins, M., 28
Tobolowsky, B. F., 24, 27, 29, 31
Trent, J. W., 24, 27, 28, 30
Turner, B., 38
Turner, C. S., 7, 8
Turner, S., 64
Turner-Musa, J. O., 38

U

Urban, W. J., 43

V

Valentine, P. A., 28

W

Wade, B. H., 27
Wagener, U., 41
Wagner, F. A., 34
Wagner, M., 28
Walker, V. S., 76
Walton, K., 32, 39, 55
Wang, Y., 34
Ware, L., 11, 12, 13, 17, 18, 22
Washington, B. T., 7, 44, 74
Watkins, W., 7
Watson, W. H., 79
Watson, Y., 43
Watt, S. K., 34, 37
Webster, D. S., 40
Weerts, D., 20
Wilburn, A. Y., 81

Williams, J., 32
Williams, L. E., 27, 32, 71
Williams-Green, J., 49
Williamson, J. A., 1, 43
Williamson, L., 63, 70
Willie, C. V., 31, 32, 44
Wilson, S. A., 38
Wilson, T., 24

Wilson, V. R., 27, 40
Wolanin, T. R., 66, 69
Woodson, C. G., 43
Wright, D. L., 28

Y

Young, H., 27, 38, 40

Subject Index

A

Accreditation: ABET (Accreditation Board for Engineering and Technology), 81–82; HBCUs and problems related to, 82–84; SACS (Southern Association of Colleges and Schools), 83

Adams Act (1906), 62

African American female students: accepted at Howard Medical School, 79; gender differences in campus experience, 31–35; marginalization of, 32–34, 53; research on campus experience of, 37; STEM careers promoted for, 33

African American middle class: black college leadership as key to problems of, 44; Obama's presidential election and role of, 1–2

African American students: anti-affirmative action sentiment discouraging, 24; current enrollment in HBCUs by, 3; gender differences among, 31–35; graduation and outcomes of, 39–41; HBCU college environment benefits to, 38–39; marginalization of female, 32–34; past research focus on, 27–28; research on campus experience of female, 37; research on campus experience of male, 35–36; research on college choice by, 28–31

Alabama, Knight v., 17–18

Alcorn State University, 19, 22

Alumni: early educating on fundraising needs of, 58; fundraising and giving by, 57–58

American Association of University Professors, 32

American Medical Association, 79

American Missionary Association, 5

Anti-affirmative action sentiment, 24

Atlanta University Center, 82

Auburn University, 17

Avon Williams Campus, 16

B

Bennett College, 33, 84

Bethune-Cookman College, 59

Biennial Evaluation Report for Fiscal Years 1995–1996 (U.S. Department of Education), 65

Black Bourgeoisie (Frazier), 44

Black medical schools, 79–80

Black middle class: black college leadership as key to problems of, 44; Obama's presidential election and role of, 1–2

Blacks in College (Fleming), 32

Bluefield State, 23

Board of Regents of Univ. of Okla., Sipuel v., 12

Brown I and II rulings, 13–14

Brown v. Board of Education of Topeka: comparing *Knight v. Alabama* to, 17–18; impact on college choice after, 31; impact on HBCUs by, 8, 11, 13, 14, 22; on stigmatization of minority students, 22

Bureau of Refugees, Freedmen, and Abandoned Lands, 61–62

C

Campus environment. *See* HBCU campus environment
Canada, Missouri ext rel. Gaines v., 12, 78
Carnegie Foundation for the Advancement of Teaching, 79
Cheyney University, 2, 5
Civil Rights Act (1964), 2, 64–65
Clark Atlanta University, 62
Classical curriculum: debate over industrial vs., 74–75; shift toward occupational focus (mid-1960s), 77; teaching and preaching focus of early, 76
College Cost Reduction and Access Act (2007), 66
Congressional Research Service report (2008), 66
Curriculum: changing global market impacting, 87; debate over industrial vs. classical, 74–75; early historic, 73; engineering, 80–82, 83*e*; evolution of graduate-level, 78*fig*–79; expanding focus on higher education, 73–74; graduate-level, 78*fig*–79, 83*e*; medical education, 79–80; problems related to accreditation, 82–84; shift toward occupational, 76–77; STEM, 33, 77*fig*, 79–82, 83*e*
"The Curriculum of the Negro College" (Daniel and Daniel), 75

D

De facto segregation, 11
De jure segregation: continued HBCU, 24; definition of, 11; *Knight* case on, 17–18
Delta State University, 22
Department of Education, 24, 28, 31, 32, 41, 52, 65, 74, 79
Department of the Interior, 73, 78
Department of Justice, 15, 18–19
Desegregation: *Brown* decision on, 8, 11, 13, 14, 17–18, 22; definition of, 12;

Fordice decisions ordering, 18–21; HBCU policies promoting, 23–25; *Sanders v. Ellington* on Tennessee's higher education, 15–17; terminology related to, 12
Dillard University, 5, 59

E

Ebony Towers in Higher Education (Ricard and Brown), 45
Ellington, Sanders v., 15–17
Endowments: low number of HBCU, 59–60; need and suggestions on increasing HBCU, 60
Engineering education: development of HBCUs, 80–82, 83*e*; federal policies promoting broader participation in, 81–82; gender differences in HBCUs, 33; HBCU baccalaureate degree awards in, 77*fig*
Equal Protection Clause, 13, 22
Executive Order 12232, 9, 67
Executive Order 12320, 68
Executive Order 12677, 68
Executive Order 13256, 68

F

Faculty: black college presidents as tyrannizing, 44; critique of governance by, 49–51; disparities of experiences of HBCUs and HWIs, 51–54; gender and racial diversity of, 47–49; gender wage gaps, 52; HBCU research supported by, 87–88; professional development and promotion of, 51–52; tenure and professional development of, 51–52. *See also* HBCU (historically black college or university); HBCU presidential leadership
Fayetteville State University, 71
Federal policies: Civil Rights Act (1964), 2, 64–65; continued research and attention to HBCUs and, 86–87; executive orders and White House Initiative on HBCUs, 67–69; Freedmen's Bureau Acts (1865

and 1868), 61–62; GI Bill of Rights
(1944), 63–64; Higher Education Act
(1965), 9, 65; Howard University and,
69; Morrill Act (1890) [Land-Grant
Colleges Act], 2, 6, 11, 62–63*e*;
promoting broader participation in
STEM fields, 81–82; Title III (Higher
Education Act of 1965), 65–67. *See also*
Governance; State policies
Fisk University, 73
Flexner report (1910), 79–80
Florida A&M's business program, 84
Food and Agriculture Act (1977), 62
Fordice cases, 18–21
Fordice, United States v., 18
Fourteenth Amendment, 13
Freedman's Bureau, 5, 61–62, 69
Freedmen's Bureau Acts (1865 and 1868),
61–62
Fundraising: alumni giving percentage of
HBCU, 57–58; comparing HBCUs and
HWIs needs for, 55–56, 59; educating
alumni early on needs for, 58;
endowment size and role in, 59–60;
history of HBCU, 56–57; infrastructure
role in effectiveness of, 59

F

Gaines v. Canada, 12, 78
Gasman, M., 6
Gender differences: faculty wage gaps and,
52; HBCU faculty and, 48; limited research
on African American students and, 31–32;
research on marginalization and, 32–34,
53; research on role of gender in college
environments, 34–35
Georgia Institute of Technology, 82
GI Bill (1944), 63–64
Governance: critique of HBCUs, 49–51;
faculty diversity and, 47–49; HBCU
presidential leadership and, 43–46;
limited faculty role in HBCU, 49–51;
state policies impacting, 69–71. *See also*
Federal policies
Graduate education: black
science/engineering doctorate recipients

(2002–2006), 83*e*; evolution toward,
78–79; HBCUs by institutional type
offering, 78*fig*

H

Hampton Institute, 74, 75
Hampton University, 59, 62
Hatch Act (1877), 11
HBCU campus environment: African
American female experience with, 37;
African American male experience with,
35–36; gender differences in experience
with, 31–35
HBCU Capital Financing Program, 66
HBCU (historically black college or
university): accreditation problems of,
82–84; baccalaureate degree awards by
field, 77*fig*; continued *de Jure*
segregation of, 24; criticism of
academics of, 44; current enrollment of,
3; examining the future of, 1–2, 3–4;
Fordice decision implications for, 21;
fundraising by, 55–60; governance issues
of, 47–54; government's definition of, 2,
9; graduation and outcomes of, 39–41;
historical origins of, 5–9; impact on
Obama election by, 1; *Knight v.
Alabama* impact on, 17–18; Land-Grant
(1890) list of, 63*e*; policies which may
promote desegregation, 23–25; post-
Brown response by, 14–15; sustainability
and future of, 85–88; *U.S. News &
World Report's* 2009 list of top, 25;
White House Initiative on, 68–69. *See
also* Faculty
HBCU history: *Brown* decision impact on,
8, 11, 13–14, 17–18; civil rights
activism by students, 9; government
commitment to supporting HBCU's, 9;
post-Civil War establishment of, 5;
religious missionary organizations' early
support and funding of, 5–6; research
understood in context of unique, 85–86;
violent history of racism as part of, 85;
white northern industrial philanthropy
financial support, 6–8, 47–48

HBCU leadership development program, 84

HBCU presidential leadership: controversy and debate over, 43–46; depictions and portrayal of, 43–44; examining context and priorities of new, 86. *See also* Faculty

HBCU research: on college choice by students, 28–31; in context of unique history, 85–86; examining experience of males, 35–36; on gender differences of student experience, 31–35; on graduation and outcomes, 39–41; need for increasing quality and quantity of, 87–88; past focus and scope of, 27–28

Higher Education Act (1965), 9, 65

Higher Education Opportunity Act (2008), 66

Howard Normal and Theological Institute for the Education of Teachers and Preachers (1867), 69

Howard University: appropriations history of, 70*e*; early professional programs at, 78; endowment of, 59; engineering program started at, 81; founding of, 62, 69; history of early curriculum offered by, 73; medical school established at, 79, 80; unique federal government relationship with, 69

HWIs (historically white institutions): anti-affirmative action sentiment discouraging minority applications to, 24; *Brown* I and II ending segregation at, 8, 11, 13–14; comparing campus environments of HBCU and, 38–39; comparing fundraising needs of HWIs and, 55–56, 59; comparing graduation/outcomes of HBCUs and, 39–41; disparities of faculty experiences at HBCUs and, 51–54; dissolution of HBCUs as remedy to integrate, 22–23; engineering program partnerships between HBCUs and, 82; faculty gender wage gaps at, 52; gender and racial gaps of graduation from, 36; HBCU's origins to maintain segregation at, 2

I

Incorporation Act of Howard University (1867), 69

Industrial curriculum: debate over classical and, 74–75; shift toward classical/professional over, 76–77

Integration: definition of, 12; HBCU policies to promote, 23–25

J

Jackson State University, 18, 19, 22

Johnson C. Smith University, 59

K

Knight v. Alabama, 17–18

Kresge Foundation, 59

L

Land-Grant Colleges Act (Morrill Act), 2, 6, 11, 62–63*e*, 81

Legislation: Adams Act (1906), 62; Civil Rights Act (1964), 2, 64–65; College Cost Reduction and Access Act (2007), 66; Food and Agriculture Act (1977), 62; Freedmen's Bureau Acts (1865 and 1868), 61–62; GI Bill of Rights (1944), 63–64; Hatch Act (1877), 11; Higher Education Act (1965), 9, 65; Higher Education Opportunity Act (2008), 66; Incorporation Act of Howard University (1867), 69; Morrill Act (1890) [Land-Grant Colleges Act], 2, 6, 11, 62–63*e*, 81; Public Law 89-106 (1967), 62; Public Law 97-98 (1981), 62; Smith-Hughes Act (1917), 62; Smith-Lever Act (1914), 62; Title III (Higher Education Act of 1965), 65–67*fig*. *See also* U.S. Supreme Court cases

Lincoln University, 2, 5

M

Measuring Up (2008), 23

Medical schools, 79–80

Meharry Medical College, 59, 73, 78, 79, 80

Military Academy at West Point, 81
Minority Science and Engineering
    Improvement Program, 66
Missionary organizations (19th century),
    5–6
Mississippi Valley State, 19
Missouri ex rel. Gaines v. Canada, 12
Morehouse College, 5, 80
Morehouse School of Medicine, 80
Morrill Act (1890), 2, 6, 11, 62–63*e*, 81
Morris Brown College, 83

N
NAACP, 12
NAACP Legal Defense and Education
    Fund, 16
Nashville School of Law, 17
National Action Council for Minorities in
    Engineering, 82
National pre-Alumni Council (NPAC), 58
National Science Foundation, 53, 82, 83
North Carolina A&T University, 6, 71,
    81, 84
North Carolina State University, 70

O
Office of Management and Budget, 68

P
Painter, Sweatt v., 12
Prairie View A&M, 6
Plessy decision, 21
Postsecondary Education Data System, 47
Private Black Colleges at the Crossroads
    (Thompson), 44
Private HBCUs: federal policies impacting,
    62–69, 81–82, 86–87; graduate-level
    programs offered by, 78*fig*; state policies
    impacting, 69–71
Professional development, 51–52
Professional-level education: black medical
    schools and, 79–80; engineering, 80–82,
    83*e*; evolution of HBCUs, 76–77*fig*;
    global market changes impacting, 87;
    graduate programs, 78*fig*–79, 83*e*

Promotion/tenure issues, 51–52
Public HBCUs: federal policies impacting,
    62–69, 81–82, 86–87; graduate-level
    programs offered by, 78*fig*; state policies
    impacting, 69–71
Public Law 89-106 (1967), 62
Public Law 97-98 (1981), 62

R
Race: anti-affirmative action sentiment and,
    24; research on obstacles related to, 35;
    segregation based on, 8, 11–14, 17–18, 22
Race conscious, 12
Race neutral, 12
Radicalizing the Ebony Tower (Williamson), 1
Religious missionary organizations (19th
    century), 5–6
Roberts vs. Boston, 13

S
SACS (Southern Association of Colleges
    and Schools), 83
Sanders v. Ellington, 15–17
Segregation: *Brown* I and II ending HWI,
    8, 11, 13–14; *Brown* on "separate but
    equal," 8, 11, 13, 14, 17–18, 22; *de jure*
    compared to *de facto,* 11; definition of,
    12; *Knight v. Alabama* on ending *de jure,*
    17–18
"Separate but equal" doctrine: *Brown*
    decision ending, 8, 11, 13, 14, 17–18,
    22; land-grant education affirming, 62
Serviceman's Readjustment Act (GI Bill of
    Rights), 63–64
Shaw College, 75
Sipuel v. Board of Regents of Univ. of Okla., 12
Smith-Hughes Act (1917), 62
Smith-Lever Act (1914), 62
Southern Education Foundation, 82
Southern Education Fund, 84
Spelman College, 33, 59
State policies, 69–71. *See also* Federal
    policies
STEM education: black medical schools
    and, 79–80; development of HBCUs

engineering, 80–82, 83*e*; federal policies promoting broader participation in, 81–82; gender differences in, 33; HBCU baccalaureate degree awards in, 77*fig*

Strengthening Historically Black Colleges and Universities Program, 65

Strengthening Historically Black Graduate Institutions Program, 65

Students. *See* African American students

Sweatt v. Painter, 12

T

"Talented tenth," 7

Tennessee Agricultural and Industrial State University (TAISU), 15

Tennessee State University (TSU), 15, 16–17, 81

Tenure/promotion issues, 51–52

Thurgood Marshall College Fund, 60

Title III (Higher Education Act of 1965), 65–67*fig*

Tougaloo College, 75

Troy State University, 17

Tuskegee Institute, 74, 75, 81

U

United Negro College Fund, 8, 56, 60, 83

United Negro College Fund's National Pre-Alumni Council, 58

United States v. Fordice, 18

University of Mississippi, 13

University of North Carolina-Chapel Hill, 70

University of Tennessee-Nashville (UT-Nashville), 15, 16

U.S. Census Bureau, 23

U.S. Department of Education, 24, 28, 29, 30, 31, 32, 37, 41, 52, 64, 65, 67, 70, 74, 77, 78, 79

U.S. Department of the Interior, 73, 78

U.S. Department of Justice, 15, 18–19

U.S. News & World Report, 57

U.S. News & World Report's 2009 list of top HBCUs, 25

U.S. Office of Management and Budget, 68

U.S. Supreme Court cases: *Brown* I and II, 13–14; *Brown v. Board of Education,* 8, 11, 13, 17–18, 22; *Fordice* cases, 18–21; *Knight v. Alabama,* 17–18; *Missouri ex rel. Gaines v. Canada,* 12, 78; *Plessy* decision, 21; *Roberts vs. Boston,* 13; *Sanders v. Ellington,* 15–17; *Sipuel v. Board of Regents of Univ. of Okla.,* 12; *Sweatt v. Painter,* 12. *See also* Legislation

W

War Department, 61

West Point, 81

West Virginia State University, 23

White House Initiative on HBCUs, 68–69

Whites: early role in HBCU history by, 6–8, 47–48; as HBCU faculty members, 47, 48; industrial philanthropy (19th century) of, 6–8, 47–48

Wilberforce University, 2, 5

Women. *See* African American female students

X

Xavier University, 59, 80, 84

About the Authors

Marybeth Gasman is an associate professor in the Graduate School of Education at the University of Pennsylvania. She is a historian of higher education, and her work explores issues pertaining to philanthropy and historically black colleges, black leadership, contemporary fundraising issues at black colleges, and African American giving. She has published many books and peer-reviewed journal articles and in 2007 won the Penn Excellence in Teaching Award.

Valerie Lundy-Wagner, an advanced Ph.D. candidate in higher education at the University of Pennsylvania, received her Bachelor of Science degree from UCLA in civil and environmental engineering and Master of Arts in Education from Stanford University. Her research interests pertain to the role of institutions in promoting success for underrepresented students and students in the STEM pipeline.

Tafaya Ransom is a doctoral student in higher education at the University of Pennsylvania. After earning a bachelor's degree in chemical engineering at Hampton University and a master's degree in chemical engineering from the University of Michigan–Ann Arbor, Ransom worked in project management, process engineering, and manufacturing supervision for a global pharmaceutical corporation. She also taught high school chemistry in Detroit and supported the development of a chemical engineering department at Dire Dawa University in Ethiopia.

Nelson Bowman III is director of development at Prairie View A&M University. As the chief development officer, he is responsible for managing major gift prospects, donor stewardship initiatives, and the university's school-based fundraising program. Most recently, he oversaw the successful completion of the university's first capital campaign.

About the ASHE Higher Education Report Series

Since 1983, the ASHE (formerly ASHE-ERIC) Higher Education Report Series has been providing researchers, scholars, and practitioners with timely and substantive information on the critical issues facing higher education. Each monograph presents a definitive analysis of a higher education problem or issue, based on a thorough synthesis of significant literature and institutional experiences. Topics range from planning to diversity and multiculturalism, to performance indicators, to curricular innovations. The mission of the Series is to link the best of higher education research and practice to inform decision making and policy. The reports connect conventional wisdom with research and are designed to help busy individuals keep up with the higher education literature. Authors are scholars and practitioners in the academic community. Each report includes an executive summary, review of the pertinent literature, descriptions of effective educational practices, and a summary of key issues to keep in mind to improve educational policies and practice.

The Series is one of the most peer reviewed in higher education. A National Advisory Board made up of ASHE members reviews proposals. A National Review Board of ASHE scholars and practitioners reviews completed manuscripts. Six monographs are published each year and they are approximately 120 pages in length. The reports are widely disseminated through Jossey-Bass and John Wiley & Sons, and they are available online to subscribing institutions through Wiley InterScience (http://www.interscience.wiley.com).

Call for Proposals

The ASHE Higher Education Report Series is actively looking for proposals. We encourage you to contact one of the editors, Dr. Kelly Ward (kaward@wsu.edu) or Dr. Lisa Wolf-Wendel (lwolf@ku.edu), with your ideas.

Recent Titles

Volume 35 ASHE Higher Education Report

1. Bridging the Diversity Divide: Globalization and Reciprocal Empowerment in Higher Education
   Edna Chun and Alvin Evans
2. Understanding Interdisciplinary Challenges and Opportunities in Higher Education
   Karri A. Holley
3. Ethnic and Racial Administrative Diversity: Understanding Work Life Realities and Experiences in Higher Education
   Jerlando F. L. Jackson and Elizabeth M. O'Callaghan
4. College Choice and Access to College: Moving Policy, Research, and Practice to the 21st Century
   Amy Aldous Bergerson

Volume 34 ASHE Higher Education Report

1. Theoretical Perspectives on Student Success: Understanding the Contributions of the Disciplines
   Laura W. Perna and Scott L. Thomas
2. Selling Higher Education: Marketing and Advertising America's Colleges and Universities
   Eric J. Anctil
3. Faculty Careers and Work Lives: A Professional Growth Perspective
   KerryAnn O'Meara, Aimee LaPointe Terosky, and Anna Neumann
4. Intellectual Property in the Information Age: Knowledge as Commodity and Its Legal Implications for Higher Education
   Jeffrey C. Sun and Benjamin Baez
5. The Entrepreneurial Domains of Higher Education
   Matthew M. Mars and Amy Scott Metcalfe
6. The Development of Doctoral Students: Phases of Challenge and Support
   Susan K. Gardner

Volume 33 ASHE Higher Education Report

1. Are the Walls Really Down? Behavioral and Organizational Barriers to Faculty and Staff Diversity
   Alvin Evans and Edna Breinig Chun
2. Christian Faith and Scholarship: An Exploration of Contemporary Developments
   Todd C. Ream and Perry L. Glanzer
3. Economically and Educationally Challenged Students in Higher Education: Access to Outcomes
   MaryBeth Walpole
4. Reinventing Undergraduate Education: Engaging College Students in Research and Creative Activities
   Shouping Hu, Kathyrine Scheuch, Robert Schwartz, Joy Gaston Gayles, and Shaoqing Li
5. Academic Integrity in the Twenty-First Century: A Teaching and Learning Imperative
   Tricia Bertram Gallant
6. Parental Involvement in Higher Education: Understanding the Relationship Among Students, Parents, and the Institution
   Katherine Lynk Wartman and Marjorie Savage

Volume 32 ASHE Higher Education Report

1. Cost-Efficiencies in Online Learning
   Katrina A. Meyer
2. Lifelong Learning and the Academy: The Changing Nature of Continuing Education
   Jeffrey A. Cantor
3. Diversity Leadership in Higher Education
   Adalberto Aguirre, Jr., Rubén O. Martinez
4. Intergroup Dialogue in Higher Education: Meaningful Learning About Social Justice
   Ximena Zúñiga, Biren (Ratnesh) A. Nagda, Mark Chesler, and Adena Cytron-Walker

ASHE HIGHER EDUCATION REPORT

ORDER FORM SUBSCRIPTION AND SINGLE ISSUES

DISCOUNTED BACK ISSUES:

Use this form to receive 20% off all back issues of *ASHE Higher Education Report*.
All single issues priced at **$23.20** (normally $29.00)

TITLE	ISSUE NO.	ISBN

*Call 888-378-2537 or see mailing instructions below. When calling, mention the promotional code JBXND
to receive your discount. For a complete list of issues, please visit www.josseybass.com/go/aehe*

SUBSCRIPTIONS: (1 YEAR, 6 ISSUES)

☐ New Order ☐ Renewal

U.S.	☐ Individual: $174	☐ Institutional: $244
CANADA/MEXICO	☐ Individual: $174	☐ Institutional: $304
ALL OTHERS	☐ Individual: $210	☐ Institutional: $355

*Call 888-378-2537 or see mailing and pricing instructions below.
Online subscriptions are available at www.interscience.wiley.com*

ORDER TOTALS:

Issue / Subscription Amount: $ _____

Shipping Amount: $ _____
(for single issues only – subscription prices include shipping)

Total Amount: $ _____

SHIPPING CHARGES:		
SURFACE	DOMESTIC	CANADIAN
First Item	$5.00	$6.00
Each Add'l Item	$3.00	$1.50

*(No sales tax for U.S. subscriptions. Canadian residents, add GST for subscription orders. Individual rate subscriptions must
be paid by personal check or credit card. Individual rate subscriptions may not be resold as library copies.)*

BILLING & SHIPPING INFORMATION:

☐ **PAYMENT ENCLOSED:** *(U.S. check or money order only. All payments must be in U.S. dollars.)*

☐ **CREDIT CARD:** ☐ VISA ☐ MC ☐ AMEX

Card number _____ Exp. Date_____

Card Holder Name_____ Card Issue # *(required)* _____

Signature _____ Day Phone _____

☐ **BILL ME:** *(U.S. institutional orders only. Purchase order required.)*

Purchase order # _____
Federal Tax ID 13559302 • GST 89102-8052

Name_____

Address_____

Phone_____ E-mail_____

Copy or detach page and send to: **John Wiley & Sons, PTSC, 5th Floor
989 Market Street, San Francisco, CA 94103-1741**

Order Form can also be faxed to: **888-481-2665**

PROMO JBXND

ASHE-ERIC HIGHER EDUCATION REPORT IS NOW AVAILABLE ONLINE AT WILEY INTERSCIENCE

What is Wiley InterScience?

Wiley InterScience is the dynamic online content service from John Wiley & Sons delivering the full text of over 300 leading scientific, technical, medical, and professional journals, plus major reference works, the acclaimed Current Protocols laboratory manuals, and even the full text of select Wiley print books online.

What are some special features of Wiley InterScience?

Wiley Interscience Alerts is a service that delivers table of contents via e-mail for any journal available on Wiley InterScience as soon as a new issue is published online.
Early View is Wiley's exclusive service presenting individual articles online as soon as they are ready, even before the release of the compiled print issue. These articles are complete, peer-reviewed, and citable.
CrossRef is the innovative multi-publisher reference linking system enabling readers to move seamlessly from a reference in a journal article to the cited publication, typically located on a different server and published by a different publisher.

How can I access Wiley InterScience?

Visit http://www.interscience.wiley.com.

Guest Users can browse Wiley InterScience for unrestricted access to journal Tables of Contents and Article Abstracts, or use the powerful search engine.
Registered Users are provided with a *Personal Home Page* to store and manage customized alerts, searches, and links to favorite journals and articles. Additionally, Registered Users can view free Online Sample Issues and preview selected material from major reference works.
Licensed Customers are entitled to access full-text journal articles in PDF, with select journals also offering full-text HTML.

How do I become an Authorized User?

Authorized Users are individuals authorized by a paying Customer to have access to the journals in Wiley InterScience. For example, a University that subscribes to Wiley journals is considered to be the Customer.

Faculty, staff and students authorized by the University to have access to those journals in Wiley InterScience are Authorized Users. Users should contact their Library for information on which Wiley journals they have access to in Wiley InterScience.

ASK YOUR INSTITUTION ABOUT WILEY INTERSCIENCE TODAY!